THE
WRITING ROAD
TO
READING

THE WRITING ROAD TO READING

*The Spalding Method of Phonics
for Teaching
Speech, Writing and Reading*

by

Romalda Bishop Spalding

with

Walter T. Spalding

Fourth Revised Edition

with a Foreword by S. Farnham-Diggory

QUILL

WILLIAM MORROW

New York

It is the policy of William Morrow and Company, Inc., and its imprints and affiliates, recognizing the importance of preserving what has been written, to print the books we publish on acid-free paper, and we exert our best efforts to that end.

Library of Congress Cataloging in Publication Data

Spalding, Romalda Bishop.
    The writing road to reading.

    Includes index.
    1. Reading (Elementary)—Phonetic method.
2. Language arts (Elementary)   I. Spalding, Walter T.
II. Title.
LB1573.3.S6   1986   372.4′145   86-647
ISBN 0-688-10007-4 (pbk.)

Printed in the United States of America

FOURTH REVISED EDITION

3 4 5 6 7 8 9 10

A PROVEN METHOD

THIS FOURTH REVISION of *The Writing Road to Reading* comes at a crucial time in American education. We have been deluged with numerous "excellence in education" reports telling us where we have fallen short. It is no surprise that many school districts are still searching for a program that teaches children to write and read fluently and to critically evaluate the speaking and writing of others.

The controversy over how to teach students to read is still raging among educators, public school administrators and other decision makers. We need to consider programs that are dedicated to the position that beginning reading instruction must include systematic, direct teaching of reading skills and vocabulary knowledge. To do less is a disservice to children and perpetuates the very serious problem of nonreaders.

In our search for a program which assured that all students could learn to read, we chose the Spalding Method. We also posed a simple question to a complex problem—Does it work? The answer was an emphatic YES! Why it works is answered in the 1985 report from the Commission on Reading, "Becoming a Nation of Readers." The Spalding Method paralleled the important research quoted in this national report.

To further substantiate that Spalding indeed works, we tracked student scores in reading and language on standardized tests. From those teachers using the method as conceived by Mrs. Spalding, the student scores ranged from 86 to 98 percentiles. I wish to add that many of these students are classified as lower socioeconomic children from Chapter I schools. Other teachers in the greater Phoenix area using this method have the same impressive results.

It is ironic that we have looked to our past to find clues to our future. *The*

5

Writing Road to Reading has been available since 1957 and is still an inexpensive and efficient method to teach our children to speak, write, spell, and read. Therefore, my message to any private or public school is that if you wish to make a dramatic difference in school excellence, start with reading and strongly consider using the Spalding Method as it is designed.

> —NORMAN L. WILSON
> Associate Superintendent
> Peoria Unified School District
> Peoria, Arizona

Our eight years' experience with the Spalding Method has demonstrated again and again the soundness and efficiency of the approach to reading, writing, and spelling. Not a single student has failed to learn to read.

> —JOHN COOPER
> Former Headmaster
> Kinkaid School
> Houston, Texas

The Spalding Method of teaching precise speech, legible handwriting, correct spelling, and accurate and understood reading has done more to provide continuity and consistency for our entire curriculum than any other factor. It provides security for those who learn more slowly and allows the others to progress further and faster. No program can compete with it for effectiveness or price.

Our eight years of use has produced tremendous results by any standard of comparison. We recommend the Spalding language arts program without reservation and invite anyone to visit us and see for himself the impact this program has made.

> —H. MARC MASON
> Principal
> Benjamin Franklin Elementary School
> Mesa, Arizona

CONTENTS

FOREWORD

by S. Farnham-Diggory*

Teach the child what is of use to a child, Rousseau said, *and you will find that it takes all his time.*

What is of use to a child interested in reading is explicit instruction in how the written language works—how it represents the sounds of speech, how it is produced with tools like pencils and chalk, how it signifies words and ideas. A program—specifically, the Spalding program—that provides such instruction absorbs children to an astonishing degree. It does indeed take all their time, or as much of it as teachers will allow.

This is perhaps the most impressive aspect of the Spalding program, its motivating power. This tells a psychologist like myself that Spalding has fully engaged the natural learning dispositions of the mind. We see this routinely in the child's devotion to the task of learning to talk. Learning to read by the Spalding method inspires a similar devotion.

Reading ability is not, however, neurologically prewired the way the spoken language ability is. There has not been enough evolutionary time for that. A pervasive error in current reading instructional theory is that children will inductively discover the rules of the written language if they are immersed in a written language environment (Goodman & Goodman, 1979; Smith, 1971). Children do, of course, discover the rules of their spoken language through simple immersion—but that is because their brains are prewired for speech. Their brains are not prewired for reading. Left to their own inductive devices, the vast majority of children will not discover how the written language works.

* Dr. S. Farnham-Diggory is H. Rodney Sharp Professor of Educational Studies and Psychology, and Director of the Reading Study Center, and of the Academic Study and Assistance Program, University of Delaware.

What they discover is that they do not understand how it works. And of course they think that is their own fault.

One of the most heartbreaking sights in American schools today is that of children—once so eager to read—discovering that they are not learning how. There comes over those sparkling eyes a glaze of listless despair. We are not talking here about a few children and scattered schools. We are talking about millions of children and every school in the nation. And the toll in young spirits is the least of it. The toll in the learning and thinking potential of our citizenry is beyond measure. The 1985 estimate by the National Assessment of Educational Progress was that only 5 percent of our seventeen-year-olds can read at a level necessary for college work. When the press first reported that number, I thought it was surely a mistake. When I read the NAEP report itself, I found I was right. It was a mistake. The number is not 5 percent, it is 4.9 percent.

The reason for this catastrophe is straightforward: American citizens are not learning to read because they are not being taught how to read. The research evidence on this point is unequivocal. The best summary of it can be found in the 1985 report of a Commission on Reading that was convened by the National Academy of Education. The report is called "Becoming a Nation of Readers," and copies may be ordered from the federally supported Center for the Study of Reading, University of Illinois, Champaign, IL 61820, at cost. Order six copies while you are at it; you will be lending them out continuously.

Fundamentally, the instructional disaster must be laid at the feet of the basal reader establishment, a billion-dollar industry that supplies every teacher and every pupil with a scheduled sequence of reading materials and lessons. The per-pupil costs and profits are astronomical. As in the case of many industries, the tobacco industry, for example, profits are not tied to healthful outcomes, they are tied to sales, and to anything legal that promotes sales. The fact that most people are not learning how to read does not deter basal sales. School systems simply switch basals, even on a statewide basis, which makes the sales game pretty exciting. But few systems have dared face the fact that none of the basals are effective. One notable exception, which I will say more about shortly, is the Peoria school district, a suburb of Phoenix, Arizona.

This is not the place to present a detailed critique of the basals, but in summary the problem is that they have lost touch (a) with the basic principles of skill acquisition; and (b) with the nature of the reading process. Details on these points may be found in "Becoming a Nation of Readers," and in other analyses by Isabel Beck (1981) of the Learning Research and Development Center—another federally supported R & D institution—at the University of Pittsburgh. A pervasive problem, for example, is that basal programs do not provide sufficient practice. A reading assignment may not even incorporate a rule that was just taught. If you understand how skill development works, and how reading works, you can easily see where the basals go wrong and where the Spalding program does not. Let me explain what I mean.

Reading and Spelling Processes

Over the past fifteen years, theories of reading have rapidly evolved from simple stimulus-response notions to complex connectionist models that are represented as computer simulations (Gough, 1972; Rumelhart, 1977; Rummelhart and McClelland, 1981). In the early 1970s, we thought of reading as a linear process: See a letter (or a piece of a letter), put it together with other letters, formulate the word, recall the meaning of the word, hold that in mind, formulate another word, put all the words together and compute a new meaning, and so on. These theories were not very satisfactory, because it was intuitively obvious that reading did not work like that. Sometimes, for example, we see a word we expect to see instead of the word that is really there. By the end of the 1970s, reading theory had evolved from linear forms to parallel forms: Many processes are now considered to go on at the same time during reading. You are forming expectations, recalling earlier concepts, picking up print, organizing syntax, checking inferences, and so forth, more or less simultaneously. Reading is, in other words, now recognized as a *complex* skill—which means that it requires coordination of a number of subskills, just as piano-playing or basketball does.

The core reading subskill is forming connections between speech and print. More technically, this comes down to connections between specific speech units called *phonemes,* and specific letters that represent them. For example, the letter *p* represents the phoneme /p/.

Spoken words are sequences of phonemes. Different words are made up of different sequences of phonemes. Since letters represent phonemes, a different sequence of phonemes will be represented by a different sequence of letters. That is the fundamental literary principle in all languages that use alphabetic systems, and it has to be thoroughly mastered.

However, a serious theoretical error currently pervades many American systems of reading instruction. It is that phoneme-letter correspondences cannot be or should not be taught in isolation because they do not exist in isolation. Phonemes change slightly from word to word. The phoneme /p/ as pronounced in the word *pot* will have more air behind it than the same phoneme as pronounced in the words *spot* or *top.* The phonemes would look different on a spectrograph. From this fact, the conclusion was incorrectly drawn that isolated phonemes should not be taught as such because they do not exist in "pure" form.

As a result, many reading programs tell children something like this: "This letter *b* is the first sound in the word *boy*." The teacher is instructed never to pronounce that phoneme in isolation. The results have been disastrous. It is simply not clear to most children what they are supposed to be learning. They do not know exactly what that letter *b* stands for, and the confusion increases as more and more phonemes are taught by this *implicit* (as it is called) method.

The children's confusion has given rise to a second theoretical error: the belief that children cannot *hear* phonemes in words—that they cannot analyze the sound pattern of a word. Of course they can if they know what they are supposed to be listening *for*.

Analogous theoretical errors would arise if we never taught colors in isolation, on grounds that colors never exist in isolation, but are always a property of some object, and are slightly different in each case. You could point to the sky and say "That is blue" and "Blue is what the rug is" and "Blue is what your mother's eyes are," and so on. You would soon have a thoroughly confused child, and you might well come to the erroneous conclusion that some children cannot *see* blue—they cannot analyze colors of objects.

In fact, it only takes a child a minute or so to learn from a color chip what color is called "blue." He can then easily categorize objects as blue, even though he never again sees any blue as pure as the color chip, or, indeed, ever sees any two blues that are exactly the same.

Similarly, children can easily learn isolated phonemes, and once they have learned them, they can easily identify them in words. Once they understand what they are supposed to be listening *for,* they can readily categorize a wide range of /p/ sounds as all being represented by the same letter *p*. The research evidence on this point is absolutely beyond dispute (Groff, 1977; Hohn and Ehri, 1983; Smith and Tager-Flusberg, 1982; Treiman, 1985; Treiman and Baron, 1983).

The fact is that human brains are prewired for categorizing sensory inputs. A sound does not have to be exactly like another sound for a child to recognize that the same symbol stands for it. We could not function on this planet if our brains had not evolved the ability to categorize a range of sensory inputs, and thus recognize that the same rule applies to them. Once you have heard one sabertooth growl, you had better believe you have heard them all.

This, then, is the core reading subskill. You have to learn which letters represent which phonemes in English. You do not have to learn every single letter-sound unit, but you need a substantial "working set." In every complex skill, there is a similar working set of basic units that have to be learned—feet positions in ballet, for example—out of which higher-order units can then be constructed. We can call the working set of letter-phoneme units the *first-order skills* of literacy.

Second-order skills refer to the fact that words are not random collections of phoneme-letter units. Some units are strongly associated with others; some units preclude the appearance of others, and so on. The skilled reader and speller knows these rules. A good instructor will teach them explicitly. It is true that second-order rules are implicit in words, and that if you simply memorized many words you will have ingested some second-order rules as well. But you will not have control of them.

One of the golden oldies of learning psychology is that rules are applied most extensively and efficiently if they are verbalizable. Once you can say what a rule is, you have maximally flexible use of it. The well-instructed literate will be able to articulate both first-order and second-order rules, as well as express them in behavior.

One interesting neurologically based difference between reading and spelling, however, is that the second-order skills of spelling are different in *format* from those of reading. When you spell, you activate your rule-knowledge sequentially. When you read, you activate it wholistically—you see a whole group of letters at once.

This means we want second-order rule knowledge to be represented in both ways in the minds of students: We want them to know that certain sounds (and their associated letters) follow others, or are influenced by others, sequentially; and we also want them to know that certain letters (and their associated sounds) are grouped simultaneously with certain other letters. You will see how cleverly Spalding has charted a path through this instructional thicket.

There are also what we can call *third-order skills* of literacy—involvement of learning and thinking processes. But these third-order skills belong to a different stage of reading instruction, as will shortly be explained.

The summary point at the moment is that the complex skills of reading and spelling require the coordination of a number of subskills, the most important being first-order subskills of pairing letters with phonemes, second-order subskills of grouping letter-phoneme units lawfully, and third-order subskills of thinking and learning.

Chall's Stages of Reading Acquisition

A helpful framework for organizing an instructional sequence for reading has been provided by Jeanne Chall (1983a, 1983b), who is the director of the Reading Laboratory at Harvard University. According to Chall, we progress through six stages of reading skill development.

Stage 0 is a prereading stage. Children are essentially discovering the world of print from billboards, cereal boxes, and the like. Stage 1 is the first stage of reading, and is characterized by recognition of the alphabetic principle—namely, that letters represent speech sounds or phonemes. Stage 2 is the expansion and consolidation of this principle, mastery to the point of automaticity, of the orthographic rules of the language. Stage 3 is the beginning of higher-order learning and thinking-skill acquisition. As the saying goes, you are no longer learning to read, you are reading to learn. Essentially, you can now develop and embed comprehension subskills in the overall reading process. You can, for example, "flag" key concepts as important to remember while you're reading along. Stages 4 and 5 involve higher types of analytical and synthetic reasoning, as when you compare points of view or use new information to modify a personal theory—all during the ongoing process of reading.

Chall provides convincing evidence that reading skill acquisition does progress through these stages, in the order described.

Strategy Training Needs

A large number of college students lack Stage 3 skills, not to mention the higher-order Stage 4 and 5 skills that college is really about. In part, the deficiencies arise from the fact that the skills were never explicitly taught. It is a depressing fact, for example, that a youngster can go all the way through a biology course in high school without ever having once discussed the text material in class. Assignments are made, and students are expected to read them and comprehend them, as demonstrated by performance on so-called comprehension tests, but not once will there have been a moment's training in the skills of understanding scientific text.

This is very serious, and I want to make clear that my current emphasis on the Stage 1 and Stage 2 training (the Spalding program) doesn't mean that I think comprehension training is unimportant. The problem is that it cannot *begin* until Stage 2 decoding is automated, simply because a reader does not have available attentional capacity.

The mind "frees up" for comprehension operations only after decoding operations become automatic. If you try to teach comprehension skills before then, you will generate a cycle of confusion: The attentional capacity necessary for mastering decoding will be drained by attempts to "remember the main idea," and capacity for comprehending will be simultaneously drained by decoding efforts. So neither Stage 2 nor Stage 3 mastery is achieved. This is essentially the current state of 95 percent of our seventeen-year-olds.

It is simply imperative to first consolidate and automate the Stage 2 decoding skills, which is what the Spalding program does, so that you can then go on to provide explicit instruction in higher-order reading routines.

We turn now to the details of the Spalding system.

Why the Spalding Program Works

The program begins by teaching a set of phoneme-letter units that Spalding calls *phonograms*. There are seventy of these, the letters of the alphabet plus some multiple-letter units like *ea* and *ng*. These particular phonograms were selected by Anna Gillingham for Samuel Orton, the famous neurologist who later also asked her to develop a method for teaching reading to dyslexics. Spalding, after teaching a child for two and a half years under Orton's guidance, developed her own method for classroom teaching to prevent or remediate writing and reading problems. (Her method is also, in my judgment, far better for dyslexics than the Orton-Gillingham method.)

An important point about the Spalding phonograms is that they are correct by modern linguistic standards. That is, the letters represent minimal speech units (phonemes), *not* blends. In many of the basals, or in other collections of so-called phonics units, children have to learn excessive numbers of essentially arbitrary letter-sound units. This misses the point of the alphabetic system: Letters are supposed to represent the minimal sound units of the language, not larger units. If you specify larger units, you lose the very flexibility and parsimony that the alphabetic system optimizes.

Learning the phonograms is a straightforward paired-associates learning task that forms tight neural links between particular phonemes, particular letters, and particular motor (writing) movements. When you master the set, you have, in effect, stocked your long-term memory with a working sample of the orthographic units of English. You can access members of this set easily and flexibly, and you can output them in written or spoken form. Learning to do this is, amazingly, great fun for students of all ages. It does absolute wonders for the self-esteem of those wounded souls suffering from years of reading failure.

After fifty-four of the phonograms have been learned, instruction in spelling begins. Spalding uses a list of 1,700 words compiled by order of frequency. Eight standardized tests that sample from this list are administered, and instruction is keyed to the threshold of a child's ability. This is strongly motivating. Easy words are boring; excessively difficult words are discouraging. Words that you can almost but not quite spell are fascinating, and discovering that you can actually figure out how to spell them is fair cause for jubilation—especially for a child with a history of spelling failure.

The spelling lesson "script" is exact. The teacher says a word and calls on the children to say the first syllable, or first sound of a one syllable word. The children write it, then the teacher writes it on the board. The child progresses systematically through the word. If there is any difficulty, the class discusses the rule involved.

Over the course of spelling, children learn by example twenty-nine second-order rules, such as the five reasons why a silent *e* is attached to the end of a word. Given seventy phonograms and twenty-nine rules, you can spell about 80 percent of English words, and a higher percentage of the most frequent ones. The spelling words are written in notebooks. After second grade, some of the rules will be, too, and again with examples. Each child thus accumulates a personal list of hundreds of words for which the spelling has been worked out and repeatedly practiced. First graders and many kindergarteners go at a pace of thirty words a week.

The personal spelling book has a remarkable psychological impact on children (not to mention parents). Most of their schoolwork disappears into teachers' files somewhere. The typical schoolchild never sees a cumulative record of daily accomplishments. A spelling book with hundreds and hundreds of correctly spelled words in it (words in the spelling book are checked to make sure all are spelled correctly) is a mighty impressive achievement. In addition, of course, the spelling book is a reference book, and children religiously use it as such. Thus, the spelling book serves as a practice, motivational, and reference device all at the same time.

In conjunction with the spelling, a simple marking system is taught. For example, both letters of a two-letter phonogram are underlined. This shows that they go together to form a unit. As another example, little numbers are used to indicate which sound is being used, if there is more than one. Thus, *mother* is marked as

moth er

showing that *th* and *er* are units, and that the second (in order of frequency) *th* sound is active. There are about five of these marking conventions. As soon as the class learns them (which is almost immediately), the students take turns marking the word they have just produced. In this way, spelling and marking works like a problem-solving seminar, with everyone deeply absorbed in doing some of the best analytical thinking of their lives.

Now you see how Spalding deals with the problem of representing second-order grouping rules both sequentially and wholistically. Once the phoneme-letter sequences have been produced (spelling), they are graphically coded. What goes into your visual memory, then, is a wholistic, graphic pattern that depicts lawful organizations of the first-order units.

When you see the word again (unmarked), it is that visual pattern, *not the sequence of sounds,* that will be activated. Thus, Spalding minimizes the risk of setting up "sounding-out" habits that interfere with wholistic word perception. Words are not sounded out while reading except rarely, when a difficult one is encountered, because they do not have to be. Structural analysis is not taught during reading, it is taught during spelling, when you have to do that sort of analysis anyway. The output of the analysis is then marked graphically, so the structure can be retrieved as a visual whole, and will not have to be sounded out again.

When about 150 words are in the spelling notebooks, reading begins. A major shock for new Spalding teachers is that reading is never *taught.* It just begins. After hours of phonogram learning, sequential word analysis, and graphic marking, children can read. They simply pick up a book and start reading. (It is, of course, a pretty exciting day.) They fly right over the basal readers with their impoverished vocabularies, and start in with good children's literature—like Sendak's *Where the Wild Things Are.* They also start right in thinking and reasoning about content. From the very first day of reading, the emphasis can be on ideas, information, forming inferences, tracing implications, and the like, because the emphasis doesn't have to be on word-attack. Stage 2 skills have been mastered. Attention is now available for mastering comprehension skills. In Chapter VI Spalding provides an overview of her approach to Stage 3 training.

By grade two, the children are reading such treasures as Thurber's *Many Moons* and Williams's *The Velveteen Rabbit.* Third graders polish off *Charlotte's Web* with aplomb. These are their *readers,* you understand. The children move quickly and deeply into the very best literature, and also into biography, poetry, and science. A list of fine writing is given for beginners through grade six in the Appendix.

But that is not the end of it. Spalding mentions that children work on her materials for three hours every day. Children in the Spalding system write stories, plays, poems, and research reports as intensively as they read.

It is very important to understand this, and not make the mistake of thinking that the richness of language arts is missing from the Spalding system. On the contrary, the richness far exceeds that found in the basal programs because the children have the skills to participate fully in the literature culture, and to pursue what interests them as fast and as far as they want to go.

The test scores on Spalding pupils are extraordinary. A sample of them may be found in Aukerman's (1984) *Approaches to Beginning Reading,* pages 541–545. The average grade-level score of the 14 first grades in his sample was 2.8; of the 16 second grades, 3.76; of the 12 third grades, 5.24—and so it typically goes on standardized tests. These scores are telling us, perhaps, what our national norms *should* be, if children were being taught what is of use to the children, rather than what is of use to the basal reading industry (Yarington, 1978).

In a remedial program, the leaps that children make can be downright alarming. When you put a logical system into the hands of intelligent children who have searched desperately for just such a system, they may run farther and faster with it than you dared to imagine. We have had children who were years below standard, reading at grade level in a matter of months—but of course they may be exceptions; only time and more data will tell.

Whatever the true success rate, it comes about because the Spalding system capitalizes on a body of psychological principles that are dead right in contemporary theoretical terms. Mrs. Spalding obviously had no way of anticipating that. Her own theoretical guidelines came from the teachings of William McCall at Teachers College, Orton's views of how the brain works, and the linguistics of the period. These theories have all been superseded in their respective fields, but the Spalding system can be recast in current theoretical frameworks because it was really derived from an intensive study of how children learn. (The same can be said of Montessori.) Of course other good reading teachers have emphasized some of the same principles. In my collection of early readers is one published in

1855. It starts out with a list of phonograms, and includes a simple marking system. These ideas have been around for a long time, but it remained for Spalding to combine them and forge them into a system of stunning efficiency.

A few words now of a more practical nature.

The Spalding Network

The system is currently spreading through a field network, rather than an academic network. Most elementary education faculty, the ones who teach teachers how to teach reading, have consultation contracts or other connections with the publishers of basal programs. It has therefore proved almost impossible to train teachers in the Spalding method before they leave college. It is after they begin teaching, discover that their pupils aren't learning to read, and discover also that *they are accountable* for their pupils' failure, that teachers begin searching for a system that works. A growing number of Spalding courses are therefore appearing on summer school and in-service rosters.

As an example of the type of field network that exists, consider Maricopa County, Arizona, which encompasses the Phoenix area. A number of school districts formed a loose consortium for the purpose of pooling information and promoting the training of teachers. Over a period of about five years, well over 1,000 teachers have been trained in the Spalding method, many by Spalding herself. The reading averages for their classes on the Iowa Tests are in the upper ninetieth percentile—and it should be emphasized that many of these schools are Chapter 1 schools, with large bilingual populations. As the need for Spalding teachers grew, the Spalding Education Foundation was formed to certify Spalding Instructors and perpetuate the method.

For information about test scores or reasons why the Peoria Unified School District in Maricopa County adopted the Spalding Method in grades kindergarten through eight, you may contact Dr. Mary Strother North, Director of Basic Skills, Peoria Unified School District, P.O. Box 39, Peoria, Arizona 85345.

Even if you are an experienced teacher, and certainly if you are an inexperienced one (or a parent), you should take a Spalding course. It makes the procedures crystal clear, and provides many tips you may miss in the manual. Here at Delaware, we offer such a course in the summer, for graduate credit. To find courses elsewhere in the country, you can write to the Spalding Education Foundation, 15410 N. 67th Ave., Suite 8, Glendale, Arizona 85306.

Acknowledgment

Mrs. Spalding and I would both like to take this opportunity to express profound gratitude to Marguerite Hoerl, a reading consultant. Mrs. Hoerl is an inspired tireless, and unswerving advocate of children's rights to literacy training, and of Mrs. Spalding's system for providing it. Mrs. Hoerl has waited with patient intensity for me to pick my pedantic way through the theoretical implications of the Spalding method, and arrive, finally, at conclusions that have been intuitively obvious to her for years. She has kept the light shining steadily on the path, and I thank you, Marge, Mrs. Spalding thanks you, and about a million children thank you.

References

Auckerman, R. C. *Approaches to Beginning Reading.* New York: Wiley, 1984.

Beck, I. L. "Reading Problems and Instructional Practices," in G. E. MacKinnon & T. G. Waller, eds., *Reading Research: Advances in Theory and Practice,* Vol. 2. New York: Academic Press, 1981.

Chall, J. S. *Stages of Reading Development.* New York: McGraw-Hill, 1983a.

Chall, J. S. *Learning to Read: The Great Debate.* New York: McGraw-Hill, 1983b.

Goodman, K. S. and Y. Goodman. "Learning to Read Is Natural," in L. B. Resnick and P. A Weaver, eds., *Theory and Practice of Early Reading,* Vol. 1. Hillsdale: Erlbaum, 1979.

Gough, P. "One Second of Reading," in J. Kavanagh and I. Mattingly, eds., *Language by Ear and by Eye.* Cambridge: MIT Press, 1972.

Groff, P. "The New Anti-phonics," *The Elementary School Journal,* March 1977.

Hohn, W. E. and L. C. Ehri. "Do Alphabet Letters Help Prereaders Acquire Phonemic Segmentation Skill?" *Journal of Educational Psychology* (1983), 75, 752–762.

Rumelhart, D. E. "Toward an Interactive Model of Reading," in S. Dornic, ed., *Attention and Performance IV.* Hillsdale: Erlbaum, 1977.

Rumelhart, D. E. and J. L. McClelland. "Interactive Processing Through Spreading Activation," in A. M. Lesgold and C. A. Perfetti, eds., *Interactive Processes in Reading.* Hillsdale: Erlbaum, 1986.

Smith, C. L. and H. Tager-Flusberg. "Metalinguistic Awareness and Language Development," *Journal of Experimental Child Psychology* (1982), 34, 449–468.

Smith, F. *Understanding Reading.* New York: Holt, Rinehart & Winston, 1971.

Treiman, R. "Phonemic Awareness and Spelling: Children's Judgments Do Not Always Agree with Adults," *Journal of Experimental Child Psychology* (1985), 39, 182–201.

Treiman, R. and J. Baron. "Phonemic-Analysis Training Helps Children Benefit from Spelling-Sound Rules," *Memory & Cognition* (1983), 11, 382–389.

Yarington, D. *The Great American Reading Machine.* Rochelle Park: Hayden Books, 1978.

AN IMPORTANT INTRODUCTION
TO THE SPALDING METHOD
by Mrs. Romalda B. Spalding*

ENGLISH is a phonetic language. It has the largest and richest vocabulary and much the widest use in the modern world.

The historian-philosopher, Will Durant, points out that democracy is the best government if the opportunity for equal education for the masses is provided. He also says civilization grows upon the study of the written records of man's past thinking achievements in philosophy. He rightly says that civilization is not inherited, that its advance depends upon the ability of each generation to fully communicate and teach its children the great heritage from the recorded wisdom of past ages. Teaching language to children is therefore the highest profession in every age. The best teaching method is of vital importance.

Nothing in all nature compares with the potential learning capacity of a young child. His teacher in kindergarten and the primary grades has an immense responsibility and an unlimited privilege of service to the future of civilization and world peace. The key to this is teaching directly with English phonics the elements of the language by accurately combining the teaching of speech, writing, spelling and reading.

The Spalding Method does just that from the start in kindergarten or first grade (and even beginning in nursery school).

For example, in spelling lessons this method always indicates the direct relationship of each sound in any spoken word to the written symbol, the phonogram, which represents it. The logic of the language is thus clearly revealed, and it is a logic so basic that the teacher can instruct her entire class as one in written spelling, whatever the individual weaknesses within the group, whether these be in the recall of the correct order of hearing, or of seeing, or of writing, the phonograms. This ability preserves the motivation of group study effort.

* Mrs. Romalda B. Spalding
3340 Pacific Heights Road
Honolulu, Hawaii 96813

Moreover, by using together all four sensory channels to the mind this method can prevent or overcome the common tendency to reverse or confuse letters, the major perceptual handicap in reading and spelling or writing. This tendency is by no means a measure of a child's intelligence; nearly all children inherit it to some extent, and fully half of a normal class will be sufficiently affected as to make beginning writing and reading difficult. The most seriously affected are often classified as dyslexic, minimal brain damaged, having a low I.Q. or a perceptual or language disability. I have found that most, if not all, such children will overcome their handicap if well taught in the Spalding Method by their classroom teacher. She will need to give them extra time and care while others in class who do not need extra drill do other tasks. The mothers of these children with difficulty should also be asked to learn enough of the method so that they can help at home. Pediatricians, neurologists and ophthalmologists are interested in the results from this method's specific, orderly presentation of the written language through four avenues to the mind, instead of only through the aural and visual.

Having been trained *first* in the written spelling of words from the teacher's dictation and having acquired a knowledge of phonics and rules of spelling, a class is able to *begin* its reading with well-written books which interest and educate and develop a love for reading and a taste for good writing.

Precise techniques for good, easy handwriting and for accurate pronunciation are taught from the very start because of the great importance of learning phonograms and words by writing them directly from hearing and saying them aloud.

Words are taught in the spelling lessons, and in the order of their frequency of use in the language (not in categories), and the important rules of spelling are taught by examples, when they are met in the writing of words being studied.

Manuscript writing is used for beginners because its close resemblance to print enables the pupil who can write a word from dictation to recognize it at a glance when he sees it in print.

The Writing Road to Reading presents in full working detail the Spalding Method for rapidly teaching children, or adults, accurate speech, writing, spelling and reading. I developed and have used it exclusively during the past thirty years of teaching in all elementary grades, in tutoring hundreds of individuals, and in giving my forty-hour course in this method to thousands of teachers. Experience shows that any child qualified to enter school at the age of five or six is able, willing and eager to write and read if he is taught by this logical approach to language. "Reading readiness" is immaterial.

The core of the method is teaching the *saying* with the *writing* of the sounds used in spoken English. Soon the child learns to combine these sounds into words he knows. Conversely he learns to pronounce a written or printed word. Meaning is well taught with the writing by using new words in the writing of original sentences.

Identical teaching is necessary for those who begin this method in any grade higher than the first (regardless of their prior instruction), although at a faster pace appropriate for their age. Parents who wish to start children before formal schooling begins can do so to advantage. Four- and five-year-olds can learn to say and write the sounds, and three-year-olds can learn to say them correctly.

All school children deserve the most effective teaching of the basic skills of writing and reading that can be devised. Without these skills the productive development of the mind, mental self-discipline and self-education, and a real appreciation of our cultural heritage are not possible. The formal education of children should be centered on developing their ability to reason, to think for themselves, and on inculcating the desire to learn. These are practical goals when *practical* teaching methods are employed. Children need and desire reasoned discipline, strong guidance and leadership from their teachers. They want to be held to high standards of performance and it will be found that problems of inattention almost disappear when teachers know the Spalding Method so well that they see and correct errors before these can become fixed in the pupil's mind.

The Spalding Method is of much help to those who need English as a second language because it makes the spelling of the language understandable and relatively easy to learn, and spelling is a key to both good writing and reading of the language. The phonograms of two, three, or four letters are symbols for only one sound in a word. They absorb most of the many silent letters and the spelling rules are equally helpful. As closer contacts expose the wide difference in wealth, religions and cultures, and consequent frictions arise, English is increasingly needed as an international means of communication as well as for better understanding between all men. Scholars estimate that three hundred million people have English as their primary language and that as many more make fair use of it. It is a required study in the schools of most countries and its use is expanding at a fast rate. This is basically because English has much the richest and largest vocabulary, simple inflections and no genders and is, except for its spelling, the easiest developed language to learn.

I am deeply indebted to the late Dr. Samuel T. Orton, eminent neurologist and brain specialist, for his years of research and teaching in the field of spoken and written English. It was my privilege while a Bronxville, N.Y., public school teacher to successfully teach an intelligent boy who had a severe writing disability, from kindergarten to the end of his second grade, directly under the meticulous supervision of Dr. Orton. This thorough training enabled me then to tutor other similar, though older, children with his guidance, and soon to teach still others by the same techniques without his supervision. He invited me to attend the series of lectures which he gave to the class of pediatricians then graduating from the Columbia College of Medicine. His theory of the functioning of the brain in speaking, writing and reading and his practical means to prevent or overcome confusions were clear, logical and highly effective in practice. His book, *Reading, Writing and Speech Problems in Children* (W. W. Norton & Co., Inc., New York, 1937) covers this from the medical viewpoint. The value of Dr. Orton's work in this field cannot be overestimated.

My contribution has been chiefly to develop Dr. Orton's training into a method for classroom teaching. The Massachusetts State Director of Special Education (speaking in 1968 at one of the nine state institutes for training in reading method teachers of perceptually handicapped children, as provided for under the state law of 1966) stated that awareness of the great need of many able children for such help was the fruit of Dr. Orton's pioneer work. Excellent results have also been obtained using the Spalding Method in public schools in New Hampshire as testified by Charles J. Micciche who was superintendent of schools in Groveton, NH.

It is important to repeat that the mental work required of each pupil in applying his knowledge of the phonograms and of the spelling rules in his written spelling builds a study habit of great value. He uses his mind and not his memory alone and thus acquires a mental discipline that will serve him in all education and in life. Another principle of the Spalding Method that warrants repeating is the importance of combining the kinesthetic skill of writing with the hearing, saying and seeing of phonograms and of words in the *spelling* lessons, and well in advance of any class's undertaking reading lessons from books. The teaching of phonics and the analysis of the sounds and the composition of words properly belongs in the teaching of written spelling. The purpose of reading is to learn what the author has to say, not to learn phonics.

This latest revised edition of *The Writing Road to Reading* meets the recently recognized need for a teacher's textbook that presents more fully and in clear detail, the long-proved Spalding Method of teaching directly by phonics the accurate speaking, writing, spelling and reading of English. It meets also the constant requests for lists of good books to use in the reading lessons.

CHAPTER 1

THE TEACHER'S ROLE

THIS BOOK is written for the professional teacher who is pleased to study in order to promote and enjoy much better writing and reading progress by all in her classroom. It provides her with accurate and practical ways to teach by the Spalding Method. The book is written without technical terms and is valuable to parents, tutors and clinics for teaching any persons who need to upgrade their reading and writing skills.

The introduction is one important part of the book. It explains the present urgent need for it and gives some of the reasons why over the last thirty years I have been teaching to many hundreds of children and later to thousands of teachers this phonics approach based on using together all avenues into the mind.

When a child enters school, regardless of his home training or lack of it, he expects the teacher to teach him and to command his attention. He already speaks a few thousand words. He finds it exciting to learn to write the letters which express on paper the sounds he uses in speaking. Inattention, even from the first day, is seldom a problem because of his vocal and written participation along with the whole class.

His manuscript writing of letters is almost identical with what he sees on the printed page. The whole world of letters thus becomes understandable and logical when he is taught to write down the sounds he speaks. He spells words by writing their sounds, and reads aloud his own writing. He uses his knowledge of phonics, his mind, instead of pure rote memorizing in both his spelling and reading.

The writing of words is the skill which most fully requires the mind to think and to direct the hand to express thoughts in logical sequence. The success of the Spalding Method, even with children with severe language problems, is in large part due to the kinesthetic tie between the voice and the hand muscles in saying and writing in sequence with hearing and seeing the phonograms.

Many schools now attempt to teach reading by the "eclectic" approach; that is, by all methods, on the theory that some children learn best by one method and some by another. There are, in fact, but two methods, phonic analysis and the whole-word or "look-say" method. The latter has caused such a high percentage of reading failures among intelligent children that it is now being nominally replaced by the all-methods or eclectic approach. The Council for Basic Education has aptly called this a "hodge-podge of postponement and readiness, questionable interpretations of Gestalt psychology, word guessing and unorganized phonics." In actual practice this comes down to the whole-word method with some phonics gradually added later on, over several years. Very few teachers have had a full course in phonics. Even if a teacher did know and had time to teach two such different methods to her class, it is not to be expected that her children could use one method without confusing it with the other.

Because it utilizes all sensory approaches the Spalding Method is so broadly based that it is effective for all pupils, including those with a photographic-type visual memory which enables them to make a start in reading by means of the whole-word approach.

It is not relevant here to discuss the objections to numerous other phonics approaches which are now presented to teachers to consider—from linguistics and I.T.A. to tape recordings, film strips, games, talking typewriters, computers etc.—but they should be briefly commented on. Most are expensive. Many aim to take over part of the teacher's work, although at the expense of the pupil's progress. They overlook the prime importance of first teaching the writing of the phonograms while saying their common sounds *before* combining them into written and spoken words and *before* starting to read books. Most of the other phonics methods teach the phonograms from printed words, and the words, therefore, are taught in categories that illustrate the particular phonogram being learned, but this is not the way words are found in literate English sentences.

The failings of most of the phonic methods may be summarized in that they neglect spelling and do not teach the saying and writing of the forty-five basic sounds of the phonograms of the language *before* trying to read.

It should be helpful to outline briefly here the basic principles and philosophy of teaching which apply throughout the Spalding Method.

The written spelling of words is in English the major obstacle to easy writing and accurate reading. The spelling may seem very inconsistent; but, in fact, it follows certain patterns and rules (with few exceptions) and basically uses its phonograms to express the spoken sounds in words.

English has seventy common phonograms (twenty-six letters and forty-four fixed combinations of two, three and four letters) to say on paper the forty-five basic sounds used in speaking it. Under the Spalding Method a class starts learning fifty-four of these phonograms by saying their sounds and writing them. Then they write, from dictation, as they say the phonogram sounds heard in each of the most used 150 words, write and read original sentences to show their meanings, and, within about two months, start reading books.

The learning of the spelling words by writing them from dictation connects at once the written symbols to their spoken sounds. *All* normal children can learn *because* every avenue into the mind is used. They *hear* the teacher say the word. Each child *hears* himself say each sound while he uses his mind in saying it and in directing his hand to *write* it. He *sees* what he has written as he then *reads* it. No other way can fix sooner or more securely in his memory the words he can write and read at a glance, thus building his sight vocabulary.

This teaching enables the many children who inherit to some degree the tendency to reverse or confuse the left-to-right sequence of letters to overcome this handicap. If a child's aural, or his visual, recall of letters is weak and vacillating, then the other three avenues to his mind reinforce it and strengthen it. Those few who can remember a word by its general configuration find this phonetic approach fully as good for reading and better for spelling and writing. They need less time on spelling, but each day's new words are taught to the whole class. All must produce, do mental work to write and read, and problems of inattention vanish under each child's desire to learn.

The average first-grade class knows the seventy phonograms, writes about seven hundred words before June, and reads many times that many. The second and upper grades learn rapidly by the same method. Classroom oral reading is centered on interesting books of *real* literature, which educate.

The seventy phonograms used have stood the test of more than two decades in use. They simplify English spelling by avoiding the teaching of nearly all silent letters, except the final e's. The latter are easily taught in this method by showing four reasons for most of them.

Precise techniques for good handwriting and correct pronunciation are permanent advantages which are taught from the start, because of the *vital* importance of learning phonograms and words by *writing* them (not by copying) *directly* from *saying* them aloud.

The whole class learns all the common sounds of each phonogram by *saying* them aloud as the teacher shows the seventy printed cards in varied sequences. (Showing together all spellings of one sound has, with two exceptions, proved needless and confusing.) The sounds of a phonogram which has two or more sounds are always said in the order of their frequency of use in words. When, in the spelling lesson, the first sound is not used in a word the correct one is identified by putting the number 2 or 3, etc., above the phonogram.

Single letters and the other phonograms are spoken of by their sound or sounds, whenever practicable, and *not* by their names.

The phonograms and all their common sounds are rehearsed until the children come to see each in a printed word as standing out as a *sound,* not merely as letters. Pupils underline each phonogram of two, three or four letters. The underlining ties these letters together as the symbol for a single sound, in a given word. Words are taught in the order of their frequency of use. Teaching the 1500 most commonly used words explains almost every spelling problem in the language. Many fifth- and sixth-grade pupils who have completed these 1500 words have made thirteenth-grade spelling scores.

Twenty-nine rules of spelling often determine which phonogram is used. They are taught as facts about the language as they come up in spelling a word and thus are learned from examples rather than as isolated facts.

The Spalding Method is direct and so organized that the children use only paper and pencil, *and* their *minds.* No games, devices, workbooks, or films are needed to teach the basic elements of English. The direct use of their minds to work and learn, and to produce on paper, is far more interesting and instructive to all children. Adults tend to greatly underestimate the mental abilities of children.

When by November the 150 most used words have been studied in the written spelling lessons, the beginning classes are ready to start reading from books, preferably from well-written storybooks of interest to their age which educate and stir their imaginations, such as the classic stories. They are not dependent on basal readers using a highly controlled vocabulary. A suggested list of books for the different ages is given in the appendix.

The teaching instructions starting with Chapter III are necessarily written for classes of beginners, whether in kindergarten or in first grade. Older students beginning with this method, regardless of their other training in lower grades, need this same teaching method and practice as do the children just entering school; but they proceed at a faster pace.

This brief outline of the Spalding Method will show how the role of the teacher makes it important that before she begins with a class she has learned the method herself. This is necessary so that she can observe and promptly correct any mistakes made by the pupils in the phonograms or their sounds, any errors in handwriting techniques or in the rules of spelling. She needs to be familiar with the book, know where to find the different subjects, and to follow its detailed directions while teaching her class.[*]

The instructions for classroom teaching or for individual tutoring begin in Chapter III following the seventy phonograms shown in the next chapter.

[*] The Spalding Method, as taught by the author of *The Writing Road to Reading,* Romalda Spalding, is available on a series of videotape recordings. For information and prices write to The Spalding Education Foundation, 15410 N. 67th Ave., Suite 8, Glendale, Arizona 85306.

CHAPTER II

THE PHONOGRAMS

THE WRITTEN or printed language is presented to a beginner as a series of phonograms, each of which represents one of the component sounds of a spoken word. This ties together logically the spoken and the written word. A phonogram is a single letter or a fixed combination of two, three, or four letters, which is the symbol for one sound in a given word. The relationship between speaking, writing and reading is constantly taught. It is the reasoned approach to any alphabetic language.

Of the thousand words we use most often, about 93 per cent are phonetic or follow the rules of spelling.

The seventy common phonograms should be so well learned that in any written word they will stand out as a series of sounds and not merely as a series of letters.

Common words soon come to be recognized as representing ideas, without the need of separating their component phonograms for reading. Writing first requires this analysis to teach the spelling. New words are studied by their phonetic sounds from the spoken word. True spelling is writing from the spoken word. This is the way of thinking which everyone must use to write a sentence. Spelling books are not suitable for teaching spelling because they do not identify all the sounds of the words, and a child who merely copies them learns slowly and by memory from his visual recall without reasoning. It develops the tendency to dyslexia.

Two-thirds of the phonograms have only one sound. Eleven phonograms have two sounds, and ten have three sounds. In learning to write a word we use numbers and underlining for such phonograms to identify which of its sounds is used in the particular word. These markings cause the child to think and help very much in fixing these important details in his mind.

We do not use the shortened spellings which the dictionary uses to show pronunciation because this is confusing and our simple markings make it unnecessary. As soon as a child can read he should learn to use the dictionary for meanings. After he becomes skilled in speaking, writing and reading, but not before, he should be taught the markings used in the dictionary for pronouncing words. It is, I believe, a serious error to introduce any of the international phonetic markings or sounds until a student seriously studies foreign languages. Speed reading should not be introduced until a child has mastered the basic and accurate speaking, writing and reading of English. Accuracy is the first goal.

This method requires of both teacher and pupil precise pronunciation of each syllable written in the spelling lesson. It clarifies the sounds for children as nothing else can. It can thus counteract the present tendency toward slovenly speaking of our language. The vowel sounds in non-accented syllables should not be indicated by the schwa (ə) and nearly all of them should be *thought of* as they are written. The precise vowel sound is lost to some extent in the rhythm of English speech. This rhythm or accent must be taught, but, for example, the word *silent* should not be taught as "si-lunt," or the word *travel* as "trav-ul." Unless we think "ĕ" in each of these words, neither spelling nor speech is apt to be precise. The influence of some linguists on speech as now reflected in some of our dictionaries and elementary textbooks should be halted by all educators.

It is necessary for the teacher to use seventy cards which show the

(*Continued on p. 57*)

phonograms in type large enough to be seen across the room.* The cards have key words printed on the back only for the teacher's information. The child learns only the sounds and the writing of them. Prove to him that the words he says are made up of separate sounds, but do not teach the sounds by having him learn key words.

Before teaching the sounds it is advisable for a teacher to check and correct her pronunciation of the phonograms. For example, the sound of "l" is not "el" but only that of the last letter, the sound of "b" is not "buh," and "k" is not "kuh." We do not say "robŭ" but only "rob." Segregate the phonogram sounds in the key words as a check on the correct sounds. A recording of these sounds is found in the pocket inside the back cover of this book.

The seventy phonograms which follow were carefully worked out many years ago and were given to me by the late Dr. Samuel T. Orton. They are still the best I have found for teaching English. The method of teaching the phonograms with the handwriting is explained in Chapter III.

Tiny babies as they lie on their backs and have eye contact become quiet as they show a fascination with the phonogram sounds.

At three and four, children soon enjoy recognizing the phonograms and saying the sounds of all seventy given in any order.

At five children learn with no self-consciousness. They do not know they can fail. They easily learn to write and read the phonograms and follow the first grade program of writing the spelling words in their notebooks. They begin writing their own sentences and reading from books.

* Boxed sets of seventy phonogram cards, 6″ × 4½″, are available. For information and prices write to Sales Department, William Morrow and Co., Inc., 105 Madison Ave., New York, N.Y. 10016.

CHAPTER III

TEACHING HANDWRITING
WITH THE PHONOGRAMS

THE TEACHING of handwriting and written spelling should precede reading from books. This is fundamental. The title of this book, *The Writing Road to Reading,* is not just a play on words. Writing and the phonograms create a wide-open road to knowing and using the written language, a road open to all normal pupils.

From the first day with a class of beginners (of any age) it is important to begin teaching the techniques of easy, legible and neat handwriting, using the phonograms for writing practice. The Spalding Method makes constant use of the control by the mind of the muscles of the voice and those of the writing hand, the kinesthetic controls, combined with the hearing and then with the seeing and reading of the phonogram the pupil has just written. This is a basic principle which is used for teaching spelling through these four combined channels to the mind—hearing, saying, writing and seeing. No other way of teaching the phonograms and the written spelling of words is so effective.

The teacher needs to have a few separated periods that give her about three hours each day for these four interrelated basic subjects: speech, writing, spelling and reading. She can win at once the interest and attention of all the class because at all times they participate with her. All must hear and learn and follow her clear, logical instructions.

All children want to do well in speech, writing (spelling) and reading. These skills are basic to our culture, and writing is the one which does most to unite and reinforce the others. Getting a child to understand and follow the mechanics of each of these processes is vital.

These lessons on handwriting, along with learning the phonograms, can help relieve tensions. The writing process is directed by the mind, which directs the pencil to perform accurately. The mind, the child's *voice* in saying quietly aloud (at first) for each letter the detailed steps necessary to write it, and the hand holding the pencil *only* to write (the other hand does *all* the holding and moving of the paper) are the only parts of the body actively engaged.

Through the years I have worked with thousands of individual children who found handwriting and spelling difficult. Their common characteristic was their excess tensing of the muscles in hands and arms and also in their legs.

The following techniques to share with beginning children in kindergarten (or younger), in first grade, and indeed in higher grades, can help teachers prevent tensions that otherwise build up.

For many years, since I learned the basic elements of this method, I have been able to prevent beginners who were clearly tending toward dyslexia from developing that great handicap. I have also by this same method rescued many older children from the frustrating failures to which their dyslexia condemned them.

Small errors prevent children from learning to write easily, legibly and neatly. They require careful and *continued* teaching of all the techniques. Children from the beginning need to be taught to follow directives. Success in these writing skills gives children great pride and interest in learning each day's lesson. Each skill builds self-confidence.

The teacher now understands the reasons for the following detailed techniques for writing. If she will learn and teach them, all her pupils will make rapid progress.

**Position and Techniques for both
Left-handed and Right-handed Children**

Clear the desk of books and materials not needed.

Sit with hips against the back of the chair, **feet** flat on the floor and **back** straight, with **head** tall.

The straight spinal column **supports** the head.

Keep two inches between the body and the desk. Lean forward just enough to see the paper clearly, but keep the **head high.**

Let the chair carry the weight of the body.

Do not let the **head** fall forward because its heavy weight then would be carried by the neck and back muscles.

Place both **forearms** on the desk with the **elbows** just off the front edge and comfortably close to the body.

The **typewriter** is a machine with two separate parts for writing. One part (the roller) holds and moves the paper and the other (the tappers) puts the letters on it. The two hands perform the two functions of the typewriter in handwriting.

The **roller hand** is the one which does *not* hold the pencil. It is placed across the top edge of the paper and moves the paper back and forth, up and down, and holds it **steady.** The paper weighs so little that little pressure from the roller hand is required to hold and move it.

The **tapper hand** is the hand that holds the **pencil** and writes.

Keep the **side edge** of the **paper parallel** to the arm of the hand that holds the pencil (like the two rails of a railroad track).

The **left-handed** child needs special attention to be sure **his paper** is parallel to his writing (left) arm. A strip of tape pasted near the top of his desk will show the correct slant for the top edge of his paper. This can keep him from turning his paper like that of his right-handed neighbors.

The writing hand and arm for **all** children should be **below the base line** on which they write.

Correct writing position for right-handed child.

Correct writing position for left-handed child.

How to Hold a Pencil

The middle finger and thumb form a vise for **holding** the **pencil**. I recommend the use of a **six-sided,** common **wood pencil** for every age.

The **pointing** finger rounds, and the end of the nail sits on the pencil where the paint ends, about an inch from the point.

The hinge (elbow) on the tapper arm should be stationary. The roller hand moves the paper enough so that the pencil point remains in a small area just forward of the center of the body.

Have each child hold a pencil across the palm of his hand and make him see that it weighs next to nothing. Train him to consciously write with no real pressure in the arm or fingers. The arm should feel as light and soft as the leg and paw of a friendly kitten. Hold a child's elbow in one of your hands and his hand in the other and have him feel no weight in his arm and hand. **Write** with the point of the **pencil.** The pencil should stand forward of the main knuckle.

All **knuckles** including the thumb should be bent and the fingers and thumb rounded to the same degree (liken this to the way a cat's claws are rounded).

Leave the space of one flat side between the pointing finger and the thumb. Run a finger between the thumb and pointing finger to make sure this is so.

Never use the writing hand to hold the paper. Make the other hand do that. The two hands have completely separate functions.

Let a little light show through under the big knuckle of the little finger so that the writing hand can move easily.

Paper for Writing

For beginners through second grade, use **paper** with **lines ⅜″ apart.** Wider spacing forces children to draw letters instead of writing. For **third grade** and above, use paper with standard ⅜-inch spacing between lines.

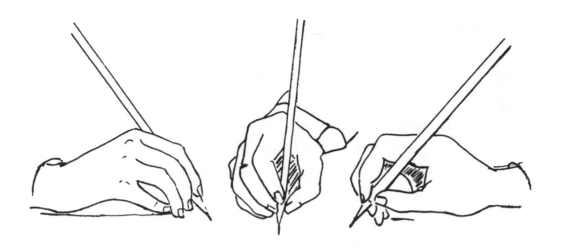

These sketches show how the pencil is held in the right hand.

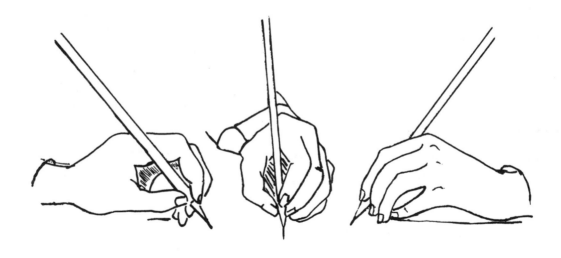

The pencil is held this way in the left hand.

Position at the Chalkboard

Rule lines on the board about three inches apart for children through the second grade. The top line should be no higher than the tallest child. Each child should write no higher than the top of his head and stand about eighteen inches from the board.

Hold the chalk with the four fingers along its length. The thumb is on the opposite side.

Write with the **side** of the point and not the point itself.

When **erasing,** start where the writing began. Begin from the top and go down, then up and down across the board.

When **pointing** to anything on the board, **stand** before (at the left) what is to be read and place the pointing finger **before** the center of the first letter. (This should also be done later by the teacher when pointing to words on paper or in a book.) The teacher can slide her finger over what is read so that the pointing finger is always at the place where the reading is taking place. This is very helpful for the children who tend to regress, or confuse, the proper direction of letters.

The Sounds and Formation of the Letters

Introduce handwriting by showing the class the printed twenty-six single-letter phonograms on the cards, in the order found on pages 66–78, saying all the sounds of each phonogram and having the whole class repeat each one after you.

Point out the differences between the print on the cards and the more simple writing of the manuscript letters. a, g and y have quite different forms in print. This familiarizes the class with both the printed and written forms and eliminates confusion when they begin to read from books. No particular order or sequence is desirable after the first lessons have introduced the alphabet.

The function of letters or phonograms in an alphabetic language is to record and represent spoken sounds. In English, only five letters, the vowels a, e, i, o and u, ever use their names in words, and their names are not their most common sounds. For example, if you write what you say for the **names** of letters in the word with, you write "double ū, ī, tē, <u>aich</u>," but the actual sounds of the letters only say "w" "ĭ" "t̸h." Therefore we use the sounds of the phonograms in spelling lessons.

Many teachers and parents fail to realize the importance of teaching the correct **formation** of the letters from the very start of teaching the written language. Unless children write correctly, they do not see the correct symbols for the sounds, and motor patterns once formed are difficult to correct. Children need much patient supervision at this beginning stage.

Teach as many of the lower-case letters in the first lesson as possible, not less than four. Review all, and teach more phonograms in each later daily lesson. Three weeks may be needed for teaching the sounds with the writing of the alphabet letters and of the other phonograms up to oa, card 54. (Teach these fifty-four phonograms to older children in a few days, as fast as they can learn them.)

Detailed Techniques for Teaching
the Lower-case Manuscript Letters

Teach the general rules governing written letters.

All letters sit on a *base* line.

Letters or parts of letters are of two sizes. They are either *tall* or *short*. Tall letters or tall parts reach to the line above but do not touch it. Short letters or short parts are **half** as high as tall letters.

Manuscript letters are made of the clock face, or parts of it, and straight lines. The teacher's chalkboard presentation will show these.

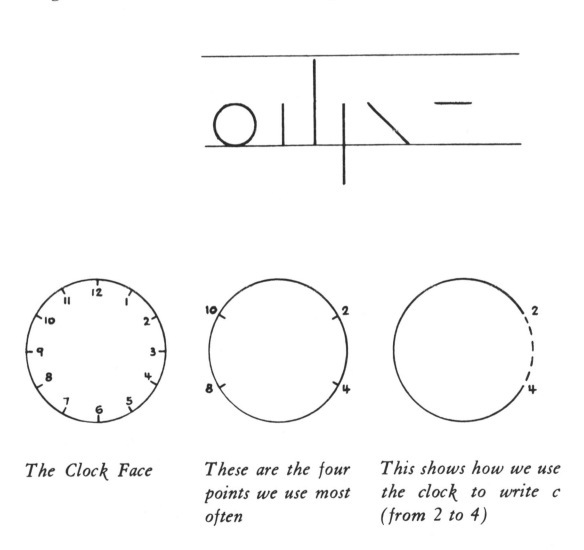

The Clock Face   *These are the four points we use most often*   *This shows how we use the clock to write c (from 2 to 4)*

Presentation of Letters that Begin at 2 on the Clock Method: Teacher shows card 22 and says its three sounds, "ă, ā, ah." (Say them in a staccato manner, not run together.)

Teacher: "I will show you how this letter is written. It is a *short* letter. Short letters fill the space halfway up to the line above. Start far enough in from the edge of your paper to make a clock face. Start at 2, *go up* around the clock to 2 and, without lifting the pencil, pull a line straight down to the base line." The class says the three sounds for a and each child writes a on his paper.

Teacher then holds up card 2 and says the two sounds, "k, s."

This is a *short* letter. It starts just far enough from a to make the clock face. (See model line on page 70.) Begin at 2, *go up* and around the clock and stop at 4. The class says the two sounds for c and each one writes c on his paper after a.

Teacher holds up card 3 and gives the sound "d." This is a *short* letter with a *tall* part. Put your finger before the round part to show that the round part comes first. Have each child feel his upturned tongue with the back of his mouth making a circle as he says "d." ("b" begins with a line and in saying "b" the lips make a straight line. The kinesthetic feel of these two letters can keep children from reversing them. Do not teach them together, however.) Start at 2 to make the short part, *go up* and around the clock to 2, go straight up to the line above but do not touch it, and pull a line straight down to the base line. This is all done without lifting the pencil. Tall parts are twice the height of short parts.

Teacher shows card 4 and gives its sound, "f." The children repeat the sound.

f is a *tall* letter. It starts below the line above, at 2. Go *up* around the top to 10 without touching the top line, pull straight down to the base line. Lift the pencil to put on a *tiny* cross in *the direction in which we write.* The cross is placed just above the middle. The left-handed child's normal direction in using his hand is away from his body (to the left). Explain this to him. Then teach him from the start that writing English requires that he makes all horizontal lines go *in the direction in which we write.* This training can save him from developing dyslexic tendencies.

Class repeats the two sounds, "g, j" (card 5).
This *short* letter starts at 2. Go *up* and around the clock to 2 and make a line down below the base line so this part is the same size as the part above the line. Round it from 4 to 8. A short letter should be able to sit beneath g without touching it.

Class repeats the sounds "ŏ, ō, ōō (card 25).
This is a short letter. It starts at 2, goes *up* and around and closes at 2.
Make it sit on the line.

Class repeats the two sounds, "s, z" (card 15).
It is a short letter. It starts at 2 on the clock, goes *up* around to 10, slides across to 4 (which is below 2) and back around to 8 (which is below 10).

Class repeats "kw" (card 13). It takes two letters to say "kw."

Both are short letters. The first one starts at 2, goes *up* and around to 2.

Without lifting the pencil make a straight line go below the base line the same distance as the round part went above the line. Make a tiny flag *in the direction* in which we write.

The second letter sits close. Begin it with a short down line, round from 8 to 4, continue up with a straight line, and finish on the base line with a straight down line.

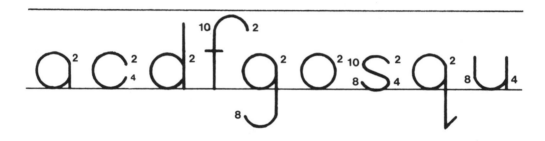

The teacher's explanation of how to use the numbers on the clock is indicated above. These letters start at 2 on the clock and *go up*. They start *just far enough* out to make a circle.

The children's papers should look like this:

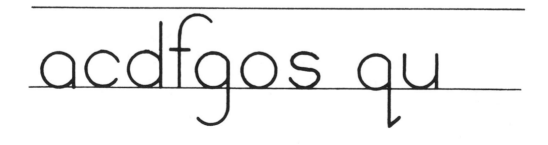

Send one row of children at a time to the board to review each day's lesson. Make sure each child holds his chalk properly, says the sounds and writes each letter correctly, and then erases his work correctly.

During the day make time to give drill to those who are found needing more attention. Seat these children near the teacher for easy supervision. For those with severe motor problems, try to teach the next day's lesson to them in a small group before presenting it to the whole class. This develops the habit of succeeding in learning as a member of the class, thus preventing the habit of *not* learning. Teach their parents *from the start* so that they can help at home. If any of these parents cannot help, make extra time in school for these children so that they do not fall behind the rest of the class. All parents should be taught the method so that they can enjoy with their children what they are learning in school.

Letters Which Begin with Lines

Teach these line letters as soon as the "clock" letters have been presented well enough to establish in the child's mind that he starts out far enough to make the circle and that he begins each one at 2 and *goes up.*

Letters which start with a line *sit close* to the preceding letter. No part of a letter is ever put before this beginning line. All beginning vertical or slanted lines start *at the top.* These are two important rules.

Do not take the pencil off the paper to complete any of the lower-case letters except in making the second part of k, to put the crosses on f, t and x, and to put the dots on i and j.

Horizontal lines, including underlining (and in arithmetic), are always drawn in *the direction of writing.* Do *not* use the words left or right. Instead establish very firmly from the start *the direction in which we write* (and read). Many remedial children, both left- and right-handed, learn to make this line correctly, but before lifting the pencil they retrace it backward. Make certain that *no* child does this, for it causes him to see the letters backward, reversing the habit which helps him learn to write and read accurately.

Class repeats the sound "b" (card 1).

It is a *tall* letter with a *short* part. It starts *at the top* with a line. (The lips make a line when saying "b.") Start just below the line above and pull the pencil down to the base line and, without lifting the pencil, go back up almost halfway to the line above and, going *in the direction in which we write,* make the round short part starting from 10 and rounding to 8 on the clock.

Class repeats the two sounds, "ĕ, ē" (card 23).

This letter is short. It starts with a straight line drawn from 9 to 3 through the clock. (Put 9 and 3 on the clock face to show this.) Without lifting the pencil, continue *up* around the clock from 3 and stop at 4.

e *sits close* to b. See the model line.

Note that e is the *only* letter for which a line is made in reference to the clock face.

Class repeats the sound "h" (card 6).

Repeat the directions for b above except that the rounded part goes from 10 to 2 and finishes with a down line to the base line.

Class repeats the two sounds, "ĭ, ī" (card 24).

This is a short letter which starts *at the top.* The dot is made last by setting the pencil above the letter and taking it off.

Class repeats the sound "j" (card 7).

This is a short letter which goes below the base line. Since it begins with a line it starts *at the top.* It goes down the same distance below the line as the short part goes above. The bottom part is rounded from 4 to 8. The dot is put on last.

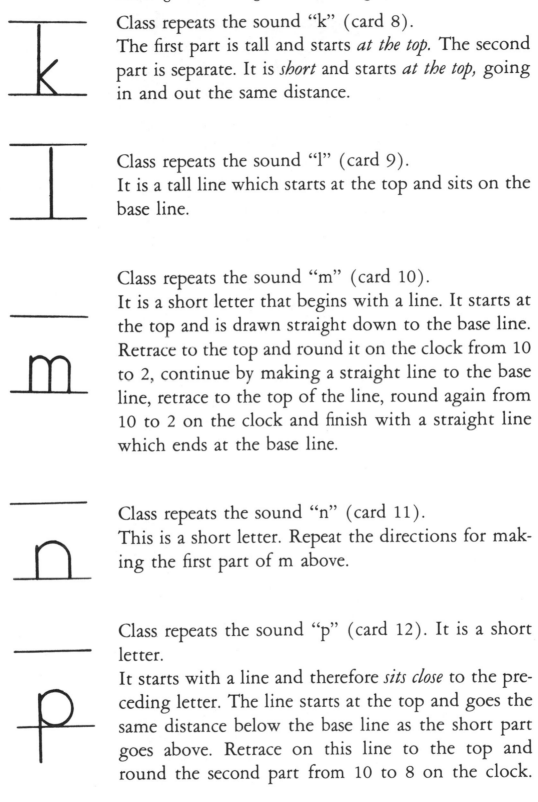

Class repeats the sound "k" (card 8).
The first part is tall and starts *at the top.* The second part is separate. It is *short* and starts *at the top,* going in and out the same distance.

Class repeats the sound "l" (card 9).
It is a tall line which starts at the top and sits on the base line.

Class repeats the sound "m" (card 10).
It is a short letter that begins with a line. It starts at the top and is drawn straight down to the base line. Retrace to the top and round it on the clock from 10 to 2, continue by making a straight line to the base line, retrace to the top of the line, round again from 10 to 2 on the clock and finish with a straight line which ends at the base line.

Class repeats the sound "n" (card 11).
This is a short letter. Repeat the directions for making the first part of m above.

Class repeats the sound "p" (card 12). It is a short letter.
It starts with a line and therefore *sits close* to the preceding letter. The line starts at the top and goes the same distance below the base line as the short part goes above. Retrace on this line to the top and round the second part from 10 to 8 on the clock.

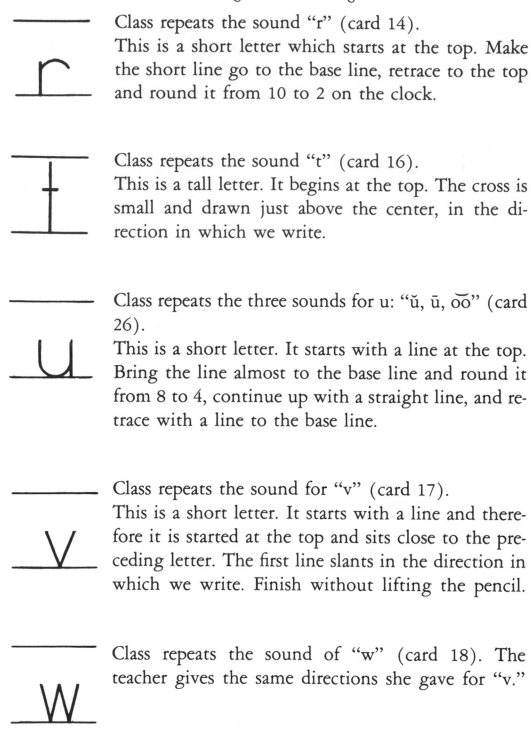

Class repeats the sound "r" (card 14).
This is a short letter which starts at the top. Make the short line go to the base line, retrace to the top and round it from 10 to 2 on the clock.

Class repeats the sound "t" (card 16).
This is a tall letter. It begins at the top. The cross is small and drawn just above the center, in the direction in which we write.

Class repeats the three sounds for u: "ŭ, ū, o͝o" (card 26).
This is a short letter. It starts with a line at the top. Bring the line almost to the base line and round it from 8 to 4, continue up with a straight line, and retrace with a line to the base line.

Class repeats the sound for "v" (card 17).
This is a short letter. It starts with a line and therefore it is started at the top and sits close to the preceding letter. The first line slants in the direction in which we write. Finish without lifting the pencil.

Class repeats the sound of "w" (card 18). The teacher gives the same directions she gave for "v."

Class repeats the sound "ks" (card 19).

This is a short letter, a line which starts *at the top,* sits close to the preceding letter and slants *in the direction in which we write.* Its cross starts *at the top* and goes through the middle of the letter. (Make sure all children write each of the letters f, t and x *before* putting on their crosses.)

Class repeats the three sounds for y: "y, ĭ, ī" (card 20).

This is a short letter. Start it at the top with a straight line, then round the bottom from 8 to 4, go up with a straight line and straight down the same distance below the base line as the short part went above. The bottom part is rounded from 4 to 8 on the clock. (As a consonant, y has one sound; as a vowel, it has two sounds and is treated as we treat an i.)

Class repeats the sound "z" (card 21).

This is a short letter. It starts with a line. Therefore it sits close to the preceding letter and the top line is made in the *direction in which write.* Without taking the pencil off the paper make a slanted line to the base line at the point under the beginning of the top line, and finish with a line drawn in the direction in which we write. The top and bottom lines should be parallel.

The teacher shows how the clock is used on the rounded parts.

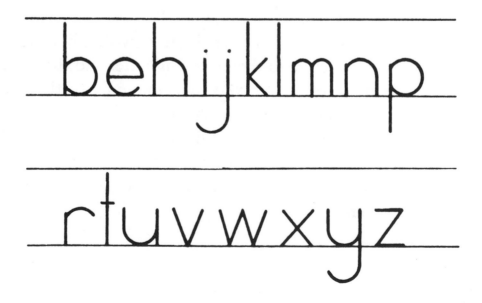

The children's papers should look like this.

I have gone into detail as to what to say to children who are learning to write because it is necessary to be specific if handwriting is to become a correct and facile tool for learning. (Cursive or connected writing is easily learned from *correct* manuscript writing. See page 84. This is done in the middle of the second grade.) If letters are made incorrectly, they are mentally pictured incorrectly also. This is a serious cause of failure in both reading and written spelling. It develops dyslexia or perceptual handicaps.

Those letters that begin at 2 *on the clock* have been taught and also those which *begin with a line*. Now dictate the alphabet by saying only each letter's sound or sounds. Children learn to say the sounds of the alphabet as easily as they could say the names. Have the letters written across the page to teach the spacing of both kinds of letters.

Letters that begin at 2 on the clock start *just far enough* from the preceding letter to form the clock. Letters that begin with a line sit *very close* to the preceding letter. The children say the sounds of the letters and also repeat the words that direct the writing of each one.

The beginner at any age in school (and at home) needs to be taught all of these writing techniques which help any child acquire the correct motor patterns. The first- and second-grade and kindergarten teachers cannot afford to skip any of them. Handwriting with the use of the sounds of the phonograms is a basic means of preventing or overcoming the confusions and reversals in spelling and in reading from which so many children needlessly suffer.

Techniques of Teaching the Manuscript Capital Letters

Be sure the lower-case letters are well learned before introducing all the capital letters. Some capital letters are needed early, such as the first letters in writing each child's name. Children should be taught the rules for capital letters and be required to give the reason each time they use a capital. When children learn that a capital is used *only* where the rules of English require it, they will not insert capitals indiscriminately.

All capital letters are *tall*. They almost fill the space between the base line and the line above. The rules for *round* lower-case letters also apply to the following capital letters. They each start at 2 on the clock and *go up*. Since these are tall letters the round parts are somewhat elongated vertically. Give the sounds of each capital letter before showing how to write it, and have the children repeat these sounds before they write each letter. The cross on the Q starts at the top and slants *in the direction in which we write*.

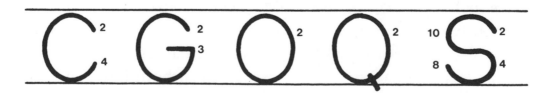

In writing capital letters beginning with lines make the vertical line first, starting at the top. The horizontal lines of A, E, F, H, I, T are made in the direction in which we write. Where there is more than one horizontal line, make the top one first (E, F, I). The pencil is lifted before making the second lines of A, B, D, E, F, H, I, K, M, N, P, R, T, and they also begin at the top.

ABDEFHIJKL

MNPRTUy

The capital letters V, W and X are made just like their lower-case letters. First make the line which slants in the direction in which we write, starting at the top. V and W are made without lifting the pencil. The second line of X starts at the top.

Y is the only capital which is finished below the base line.

Z is formed the same as its lower-case letter. The top line is drawn in the direction in which we write and it is finished without taking the pencil off the paper.

Techniques of Teaching Numbers

All numbers should be made halfway between the size of a short letter and a tall letter.

The numbers 8, 9 and 0 begin at 2 on the clock. Since they are taller than short letters, elongate them somewhat vertically.

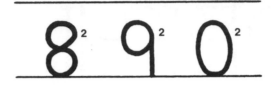

The rule for the spacing of numbers which begin at 2 on the clock is the same as for manuscript letters. Start just far enough away to make a clock.

The numbers 1, 4, 5 and 6 begin with a line and all lines start at the top. The left-hand vertical line of 4 is written first. The horizontal line of the 5 is short and is drawn last and in the direction of writing.

The bottom of a 6 can end on the base line. Then it never looks like 0. 7 begins with a line drawn in the direction of writing.

The numbers which begin with a line sit very close to the preceding number. This is also true for 2 and 3.

A parenthesis, a question mark, an exclamation mark, quotation marks and an apostrophe are started at the same height as the numbers.

Numbers 2 and 3 begin at 10 on the clock. Note that no lowercase letter starts at 10 so these two numbers should be thoroughly understood by children who show confusion in direction.

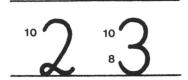

Now write all the numbers on a line showing the proper spacing. All except the last three, which begin at 2 on the clock, start close to the preceding number. Numbers should be thought of as sitting between parallel lines.

1234567890

Before the children write 2 and 3 ask where these two numbers start until every child knows they begin at 10 on the clock. (Children who reverse these numbers can come to dislike arithmetic. It is very important to prevent this reversing.)

In itemizing or numbering pages, I do not put periods after whole numbers. In mathematics a period is a decimal point and it is read "and." 5.2 is read "five and two-tenths."

In writing the brain directs the hand. This cannot be done correctly unless there is a thorough knowledge of how each letter and number is made.

The child who has no difficulty in learning to write needs to be taught at first, but need not be held for drill. The children who need help should be given the specific directions in this chapter over and over until they can direct their hands in writing and no longer make errors in direction or orientation. This is where drill is an essential part of teaching, if children are to learn. The teacher has done no teaching unless and until the pupil learns.

After the first presentation, it is well to have small groups, in turn, write at the chalkboard. Errors in writing can thus be readily caught and corrected.

After teaching the sounds and the writing of single manuscript letters the teacher presents all the other phonograms on the seventy cards in varying sequences, but in the same manner as the single letters were presented. The phonograms now should be written in two columns down the page rather than across the page. Have the children fold their papers down the middle and use the crease to line up the second column. The phonograms must be thoroughly learned with the accurate sounds and they must be correctly written (not copied).

Spacing has already been shown so that when a card of more than one letter is written the question "Where does the second or subsequent letter start?" should bring the response, "At 2 on the clock. Start just far enough out to make a clock," or, "It begins with a line which sits close to the last letter. A line starts at the top."

When words are introduced the spacing of letters within a word follows the above rules. A space the size of one round letter is left between words. (Show the children that on the typewriter, pressing the space bar once leaves such a space.) Children's papers are more easily read if they leave the space of two letters between sentences.

After children can easily form the letters correctly they should learn to reduce the size of their handwriting. This reduced size is used in showing the cursive writing which follows.

Cursive Writing

Cursive writing follows the same rules for position as those given for manuscript writing.

The letters of connected (i.e., cursive) writing should be taught only after manuscript writing with the phonogram sounds has been perfected and no longer requires any special attention. This can be after Christmas in the second grade. Children want to learn cursive writing. A promise to teach it as soon as they perfect the basic manuscript writing is an incentive to a real effort to improve.

All the letters within a word in cursive writing are connected.

The connecting lines from the end of one letter to the right place to start the next letter are of five kinds:

⟋   a short upswing from the base line

⟍   a tall upswing from the base line

⌒   a short upswing which curves over to 2 on the clock

⌣   a short dip kept at the height of a short letter across to the start of the next letter, or as a tiny ending on the letters b, o, v and w

∿   the short dip that curves over to 2 on the clock

Vertical lines that start at the top are drawn straight down.

All letters which go below the base line and curve back up cross at the *underside* of the base line at the point where the down line crossed the base line.

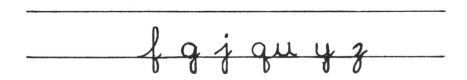

The vertical lines in cursive writing can be slanted forward for the right-handed child. All such lines are parallel to each other. Left-handed writers can write straight up and down. If they develop a slant it must be backhand, never forward.

Most of the differences between manuscript and cursive writing are shown by the dotted lines in the cursive letters below. The solid lines show to what extent the letters are alike.

abcdefghijklmnopqrstuvwxyz

abcdefghijklmnopqrstuvwxyz

Cursive writing is easily taught by having the children write the entire manuscript alphabet and then write over it the cursive letters with connecting lines and other changes, as shown above. The differences are readily seen. Be sure all the sounds of each letter are spoken just before it is written.

acdghijlmnopqu tuvwxy

b e f k r s z

The forms of a, c, d, g, h, i, j, l, m, n, o, p, qu, t, u, v, w, x and y are essentially the same in cursive writing and in manuscript. The letters b, e, f, k, s and z are changed the most, and need more attention.

v and w are written the same as in manuscript except that the lower sharp points are rounded and they end with a dip at the top.

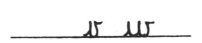

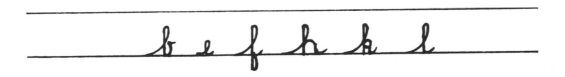

b, e, f, h, k and l start with an upswing which makes a sharp curve backward at the top to start the straight down line.

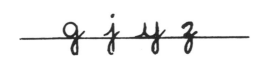

g, j, y and z are the letters which end with a straight line down below the base line and take a sharp curve backward at the bottom and up to connect to the next letter. This up curve crosses the down line exactly at the base line.

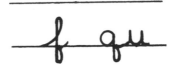

f and q turn forward and swing up, meeting the down line exactly at the base line. The q turns at the bottom as did the flag in the manuscript form.

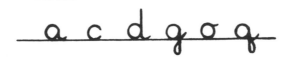

d and p have no loops.

a, c, d, g, o, and q, letters which in manuscript begin at 2 on the clock, also can begin at 2 in cursive writing when they are the first letters of words.

m, n, u, v, w, x, and y may also be made without an initial up line from the base line at the beginning of a word.

m, n and x need **special** attention. Round into the down lines for m and n. The first down line is the same as the *first down line of the manuscript letter*. Round into the slanted down line of the x. This is the *same letter as the manuscript form* and the cross is still made from the top through the center of the letter.

All down lines are *straight* lines. When they are slanted the slant should be the same for each down line. The right-handed slant slightly forward. The left-handed slant slightly backhand.

All letters at the end of a word or when written alone end with a short upswing from the base line except b, o, v and w, which end with a dip, the beginning and end of which is kept at the height of a short letter.

Spacing between words should be closer in cursive than in manuscript writing because the end of a word is shown by the absence of a connecting line to the first letter of the next word.

Drill at the chalkboard is essential for those who do not show facility in learning at the time of the first presentation.

Once connected writing is introduced, do not let the pupils use manuscript writing again in spelling, compositions, etc. As soon as the connected alphabet is taught, teach the writing of the rest of the seventy phonograms. Then review the Extended Ayres List of words so that all the possible connections can be shown. The phonograms wor, ow, ou, oi, oy, oo, wh, oa, wr and oe need special attention. The second letter does not start with an upswing from the base line. The rest of it is put on the end of the dip which remains on a level with the *beginning* of the dip. be, op, wi, we, ol, bu, bo, by, ve and ot have connections that need to be explained when the words in Sections A–H are dictated.

The Capital Letters in Cursive Writing

Certain capital letters in cursive writing do not connect to the next letter. These are D, F, O, P, V and W.

The capital letters D, E, F, T, G, I, J, L and Q are different forms from their lower-case letters or manuscript letters.

D starts with a straight down line and is completed without lifting the pencil.

E and L begin at 2 on the clock.

I and J are the only letters that begin at the base line with a backward upswing and curve forward at the top. (All upswings for lower-case cursive letters are forward.) I and J should be carefully taught together. As lower-case letters they are the only ones which are dotted. As capitals they are the only ones that begin with a backward upswing.

G and S start alike with an upswing from the base line.

T and F begin with a dip at the top.

Q and Z begin at 10 on the clock as do the numbers 2 and 3.

Other Writing Hints

A comma is a *tiny* half-clock. It starts on the line comfortably close to the letter it follows, and goes below the line rounding from 12 to 6 on the clock.

When the children first write a period, say, "A period is made by setting the pencil on the line comfortably close to the letter it follows, and taking the pencil up." This keeps children from setting commas and periods just any place, and also gives a precise kinesthetic feel to them. It also helps them to see commas and periods on the printed page. Also see page 258.

I am convinced that teachers must demonstrate and explain much more about how each letter, number and punctuation mark should be formed and placed. The strange, awkward ways in which nearly all children contrive to form some of their letters show their need of all these techniques of handwriting.

The first letter written on a page should be written carefully because every letter that follows should be of the same relative size.

Every round letter should fit on the same-sized clock.

Tall letters and capitals are twice as high as short letters.

All letters which go below the base line go just as far below the base line as short letters go above it.

I have given a great deal of study to the techniques of teaching good and easy handwriting, not only for its own sake but also for the facility for self-expression and for clarifying of one's ideas that comes from a command of easy, readable writing. The prime reason is that it is the simplest direct means of learning the sounds of English as they are represented in our written language. I do not know of another book on handwriting which at every point ties in the *sounds* of the letters with their forms. And yet what meaning can the form of a letter have unless it conveys its sound to the child as he learns to write it? This is one of the reasons why writing is the logical road to reading.

CHAPTER IV

SPELLING RULES AND
THE NOTEBOOK

THIS CHAPTER demonstrates in detail the method by which each child above the second grade writes the first seven pages in his own notebook every year. It is his own reference book for the phonograms and for the rules of spelling and pronunciation.

Spelling rules, explanatory notes and instructions for the teacher are given along with each page of the model of the first seven pages of the notebook.

The teachers in the first and second grades, as well as those in the upper grades, need to be fully conversant with this entire notebook and its explanations in order to teach and explain correctly any word that comes up in speech, writing or reading.

It should be noted here that Pages 1, 2, 5, 6 and 7 of the Notebook are basic. Their contents are taught in all grades even though the children in the first two grades do not write all of this part in a notebook.

I want to emphasize that the teacher or parent who gives careful attention to the procedure and meticulously follows all the major and minor details of teaching for the mental and physical production of this notebook will be well rewarded. Progress of each and all of her pupils will henceforth make her work much lighter and a source of pleasure. The mastery of the notebook is one key to the pupil's success in his use of the language arts. This is where competent teaching really counts.

In presenting the writing of the notebook to the third grade and each higher grade, the teacher should explain the purpose of the notebook. Many classes of high-school students and many people of college age and older have needed it and have written its pages.

Teach manuscript writing at first to each student no matter what his age. The older student needs manuscript for lettering maps, diagrams and drawings, but chiefly it makes a needed visible link between his writing and all printed matter. Older students should write the phonograms given on the cards and the words of the Ayres Word List to Section O in manuscript. This gives them a kinesthetic connection between the sounds and printed forms for reading. For those with any reading handicap this is highly important.

Third grade and all older students write the first seven pages of the notebook in cursive writing.

Detailed Technique for Teaching Page One

The first page lists the single consonants at the top. It gives the single vowels and words to show the important sounds of each vowel. At the bottom of the page are listed the five kinds of silent final e's.

The teacher says that the first word "Consonants" is the title or name for the next line of letters. The word Consonants goes in the middle of the top line. Since it is a title, we write it with a capital. We divide it into syllables.

A syllable is that part of a word or a single word which is capable of being pronounced by a single impulse of the voice. Once when teaching a group of ninth-grade boys who had no idea what a syllable was I used my hands to indicate the beat of the syllables. Take the word Consonants. After the class says "Con" the teacher, facing the class, makes a down beat with her right hand. The class says "so" and her left hand makes a down beat. For "nants" she crosses the right over the left for the final beat. The pupils, in showing syllables in this manner, start with the left hand, then the right and then the left crossed over the right hand. This kinesthetic effect has proved helpful to many and can even be used with preschool children to establish correct pronunciation.

A pupil who is not sure which hand represents the first syllable can stand before the word written in syllables on the chalkboard and lay his hand on the first syllable and the other hand on the second one. This physical feel is very necessary for some. Do not confuse by calling his hands left and right. Establish which hand represents the first syllable by having him hold it up.

To go a step further in the kinesthetic feel of a word the teacher holds up three fingers of her right hand, showing that it takes three letters to write the first syllable, and points to the finger on her right. The children say the sound "c"; as she points to the next finger they say "ŏ"; and as she points to the next one they say the sound "n." Then the teacher holds up two fingers of her left hand. She points to the one to her right and the children say the sound "s." She then points to the other finger and the children say "ō," showing there are two letters to write so. Then crossing the right hand over the left, she holds up five fingers for nants and points to each in turn as the children give the individual sounds.

A teacher facing her class can, in her mind, project her right hand against the board behind her and know her right hand should represent the first syllable. With her palm toward the class her little finger represents the first letter of a syllable behind her. Many teachers as well as many students have some difficulty in orientation.

These procedures give children who have difficulty learning to spell a chance to think what the writing must be, before they actually write. Such reasoning keeps children from making errors which once made must be supplanted later. This is good teaching.

The teacher asks the class to give her the first syllable of Consonants. When she gets the reply "Con," she writes it on the board. At the same time the children are writing it in their notebooks. (They write while she is writing because they are *not* to copy her writing.)

While writing Con, the teacher asks for the second syllable. When she gets the reply "so," she puts it on the board while the children write it their books. While writing so, the teacher asks for the third syllable. When she gets the reply "nants," they write nants while she writes it, and they sound out "n," "ă," "n," "t," "s." This helps them to write it accurately. This sounding of the phonograms should always be done with any syllable which presents a difficulty in accurate pronunciation or in writing.

The teacher then says, "On the next line we will write the single consonants." (These are printed in order on the first twenty-one phonogram cards.) She asks, "The first consonant in the alphabet says what?" The class gives the sound "b" (not "bŭ") and writes the letter. For c they say "k," "s" for the two sounds of c and write the letter c. (Since no consonant ever uses its name for its sound, we never say the names of these letters when it is possible to use their sounds instead.)

The class should know the phonograms and give the sounds in unison. Before they write, they are reminded of how each letter is made in case any child is not sure of it. Continue writing the rest of the consonants in the same manner.

On the third and fourth lines write, "c before e, i or y says $\overset{2}{c}$. If g is before e, i, or y, it may say $\overset{2}{g}$." The teacher has the children say and write each of the phonograms in these words as they are written. She will have previously studied the Extended Ayres List which begins on page 133 and will know how to teach these words just as described. The above description of writing the word "Consonants" is identical with this, except that in one-syllable words each phonogram is sounded before it is written.

The teacher tells what is to be written and where. Everything which is written must also serve as continued training in the accurate writing of the sounds and sequences of speech.

On the next line the class writes the title "Vowels" using exactly the same procedure as described for the title "Consonants." Here we put a 2 above the s. In this case and where figures above phonograms may be written hereafter, the figure above a phonogram indicates that the word uses the phonogram's second sound or the third, etc. These sounds are always numbered in the sequence as listed on the backs of the phonogram cards. When no figure is written above, it signifies that the first sound is the one used in the word. (Numbers are not needed above the phonograms c and g because simple rules tell which sound to use.)

The single vowels are on the phonogram cards 20, and 22 to 27.

The five kinds of silent final e's have a special way of being underlined and numbered. On all seven pages of the Notebook and also in the Extended Ayres List of 1700 words, all these silent final e's are identified by underlines and the numbers 2, 3, 4, or 5 written *below* base lines just after the double underlines. If the e belongs to the first kind of silent e, no number is put under it.

The other pages of the Notebook should be presented in the same manner as described above.

Notes to Teachers about Page One

This page presents the twenty single-letter and the two-letter qu consonants, the six single-letter vowels, and the five kinds of silent final e's.

This is a spelling notebook. In it words when written alone are divided into syllables so that the relationship between the sounds and the symbols can be readily seen.

Each consonant has but a single sound except c, g and s. Rules 2 and 3 below make it unnecessary to number the second sounds of c and g. Only s when it says "z" needs a 2 placed above it when learning to pronounce and write words.

Avoid using the terms "name" of a letter, "the long vowel," or "short vowel." Instead use the sound itself because the other words are only names for sounds and are thus less direct.

The pupils must learn to understand and apply the following seven rules.

Rule 1. q is always written with two letters qu when we say the sounds "kw." The u is a consonant here.

[See text pp. 93–96]

A model of Page One
of the Notebook.

Con so nants

b c d f g h j k l m n p qu r s t v w x y z

c before e, i or y says ç, and

if g is before e, i or y it may say g̊

Vowels

a	at	na vy	want
e	end	me	
i	{ In di an	si lent	
y	{ ba by	my	
o	odd	o pen	do
u	up	mu sic	put

Silent final e's { time
have   blue
chance   charge
lit tle
are   (no job e)

Rule 2. When c by itself has a sound, it always says "s" if followed by e, i, or y (cent, city, cyclone); otherwise its sound is "k" (cat, cyclone, music).

In many words ci is pronounced "sh," and then it is a two-letter phonogram and thus does not have either sound of c. ch is always a two-letter phonogram. Rule 2 applies only where c is a single phonogram.

Rule 3. When g has a sound by itself it can say "j" only if it is followed by e, i, or y. When followed by any other letter, it says "g." (Get, girl and give show that e and i do not always make g say "j.") In spelling if g is used to say "j," it must be followed by e, i, or y, as in pigeon, religious, energy.

These rules 2 and 3 are most valuable. They enable the child to know the correct sound for c and g by means of the letter that follows. The teacher should ask for these rules until the children apply them automatically, in both writing and reading. These are the only letters in the alphabet affected in sound by the letter which immediately follows.

The single vowels are underlined in words only when they say ā, ē, ī, ō. ū at the end of a syllable. y like i is also underlined when it says ī. Teach the sounds of the vowels in the order given. The first one is used most frequently.

Rule 4. Vowels a, e, o, u usually say "ā," "ē," "ō" "ū" at the end of a syllable: (na vy, me, si lent, my, o pen, mu sic.) This is one of the three ways a vowel may say ā, ē, ī, ō, or ū.

Rule 5. i and y can say "ī" at the end of the syllable but usually they say "ĭ." This is shown at the end of the second syllable of both Indĭan and babў.

Rule 6. y, not i, is used at the end of an English word, except for the pronoun I.

Rule 7. There are five kinds of silent e's. In short words, as me, she, he, the e says "ē," but in longer words where a single e appears at the end, the e is silent. (There are very few exceptions.) In Chaucer's day they were sounded. Now they are silent. As shown below we retain the first four kinds of silent e's because we need them. The fifth kind is probably a relic from Chaucerian days.

The Five Kinds of Silent Final e's

1 t<u>ime</u>. This is an "ī," then a consonant and a final e. Pupils underline and say "ī," "m," "ē." The silent e is put there to let the i say "ī" instead of ĭ. This is true in <u>late</u>, <u>here</u>, st<u>yle</u>, r<u>ose</u>, t<u>une</u>. The single vowels before any single consonant can say "ā," "ē," "ī," "ō," or "ū" if a silent e follows to end the base word. (Sometimes there are two consonants between as in <u>paste</u> or b<u>athe</u>. These words are past and bath when the silent e is omitted.)

2 ha<u>ve</u>₂, bl<u>ue</u>₂. In English we cannot end a word with v or the single vowel u. We add a silent e. (Impromptu is one of the few exceptions.)

3 chan<u>ce</u>₃, char<u>ge</u>₃. The silent e follows c and g so they can say "s" and "j." Without the e, the last sounds would be "k" and "g." Rules 2 and 3 show this.

4 lit t<u>le</u>₄. Every syllable in English must contain at least one vowel. b<u>le</u>₄, c<u>le</u>₄, d<u>le</u>₄, f<u>le</u>₄, g<u>le</u>₄, k<u>le</u>₄, p<u>le</u>₄, s<u>le</u>₄, t<u>le</u>₄, and z<u>le</u>₄ are the only syllables where neither of the first two letters is a vowel and the silent e is added in each so they can be separate syllables. All other syllables in English have a vowel sound.

5 <u>are</u>₅. The e is not needed for any of the above reasons. It has no job and we call it the "no job e." H<u>ouse</u>₅, co<u>me</u>₅, promi<u>se</u>₅ are other examples of silent e's which perform no useful purpose in present-day English.

All of the above facts about our language can be learned from Page one. The teacher should make constant reference to this page and to the six pages that follow to illustrate facts about our language as the pupils learn to write and read. This gives them understanding and security in speaking, writing and reading.

After each time words are written in the notebooks, they should be collected, opened to the page to be checked. One after another the students come to your desk to make the necessary corrections. If this is done from the first day, very soon there should be no errors.

Notes to the Teacher about Page Two

<u>He</u>r f<u>ir</u>st n<u>ur</u>s<u>e</u>₅ w<u>or</u>ks <u>ear</u>ly.

This sentence gives five spellings of the sound "er" and it should be memorized. Their phonogram cards are numbered 27 to 32. The spelling er is used most often.

Rule 8. or may say "er" when w comes before the or, as in works. There are few other guides in the choice of the spelling of the sound "er."

First dictate the model sentence containing the five spellings of the sound "er." It sits on the top line of this page. Teach each word as described for teaching words on Page one. Skip the second line. Then dictate the five words across the third line, and so on.

Check the children's knowledge of this page by asking, for example, "Which 'er' is in church?" The answer is, "The one in nurse." (See the model sentence at the top of the page.) Do this same checking with any word having an "er" sound.

Consider, in other words such as doctor and collar, or and ar as having only the sounds as in for and far. In writing them say "doc t<u>or</u>" and "col l<u>ar</u>."*

The words service, nervous and rehearsal are explained on Page 6 of the Notebook. The base word of h<u>ear</u>d is h<u>ear</u>.

---

* This can eliminate the use of the schwa which deteriorates unaccented vowels to "ŭ," the lowest sound we have. The schwa does not appear in the Oxford Dictionary and did not appear in the United States dictionaries until after 1957 when some linguists introduced it.

The y having the sound "ē" was introduced at the same time. However i and y (as a vowel) have always been interchangeable. In saying family as "fam ē lē" we distort speech and make learning to spell more difficult. As an educator I do not accept either the schwa or the y having an "ē" sound.

Her	first	nurse =5
fern	third	hurt
herd	bird	burn
din ner	girl	church
berth	birth	turn
west ern	fir	fur
merge =3	thirst	pur pose =5
perch	firm	hur dle =4
gro cer y	squirm	sur prise
serv ice =3	squirt	{ Thurs day
verse =5	chirp	{ Sat ur day
{ nerve =2	cir cle =4	fur ther
{ nerv ous	sir	oc cur
ster ling	con firm	fur nish
per fect	skirt	dis turb
clerk		sub urb
cer tain		cur tain

works | ear ly.

worm	learn
word	heard
world	search
worth	earn
wor thy	ear nest
worse	pearl
worst	earth
wor ry	re hears al
wor ship	

[See text p. 102]   We use ei after c, — — — — — —

ie	cei
be lieve	re ceive
be lief	per ceive
fierce	ceil ing
brief	re ceipt
niece	con ceit
priest	
field	
siege	
friend	
chief	
a chieve	
piece	
pie	
lie	
prai rie	
lil ies	

if we say "ā," ————— and in some exceptions. A model of Page Three
of the Notebook.

ei says "ā"	Exceptions	
their (they)	Nei ther	
veil	for eign	
skein	sov er eign	Learn
heir (in her it)	seized	this
rein	(the) coun ter feit	as a
reign	(and) for feit ed	sentence.
vein	lei sure.	
sur veil lance		
	ei ther	
	weird	
	heif er	
	pro tein	

Notes to the Teacher about Page Three

First dictate the four headings of the columns. Skip a line. Then dictate and on the third line write the top word of each of the first three columns, then the three words on the line below and so on. Then dictate the exceptions in the fourth column from top to bottom. Children readily learn the nonsensical sentence given and learn that all these words plus the few at the bottom of the column contain ei. From the headings on this page it can be seen that there are three places for the use of the phonogram ei. The cards 56 and 57 show the three sounds each for ie and ei and two of these are the same for both phonograms. Therefore the sound alone cannot show which of these spellings to use. Rule 9 tells which phonogram to use. It is necessary here to say the names of the letters ie and ei.

Rule 9. After c we use ei. If we say "ā" we can use ei, never ie. In the list of exceptions we use ei. In all other words that contain ie or ei we use ie.

---

ie says "ĕ" in friend. Put two lines under it. These double lines are used to mark any such phonogram which has an uncommon sound that is not given on the phonogram cards. ie follows Rule 9.

eigh is not considered on this page because this phonogram should say "ā." It is not ei alone. In foreign the ei says "ĭ" and the gn says "n." They are not one sound as is eigh.

The teacher tests each child by asking which spelling, ie or ei, is used in the listed words. Example: Which is used in receive? In answering the child should say "ei because it comes after c"; or, if the word is brief, he will say "ie because it comes after 'r' and not after c, the sound is not 'ā,' and it is not one of the exceptions."

If students, in this way, apply and state these rules often enough they will use them when they write. It is the old problem of learning to think before they write or speak. It helps them develop the vital habit of using their minds in what they do and say.

Notes for the Teacher about Page Four

This page explains the usual spellings for the sound "sh" at the beginning of any syllable after the first one. Cards No. 67, 68 and 69 show these.

Dictate these words, after the column headings and a general discussion of Rules 10 through 13, by going from top to bottom of each column in turn. (Be sure the words are dictated as said in conversation, but that the children say each separate syllable just before they write it in their notebooks.)

Rule 10. sh is used at the beginning or end of a base word and at the end of a syllable (she, finish) but, except in the ending ship (friendship, worship), it is not used at the beginning of a syllable after the first one in a base word.

Rule 11. ti, si and ci are the phonograms most frequently used to say "sh" at the beginning of a second or subsequent syllable in a base word.

Rule 12. si is used to say "sh" when the syllable before it ends in s (ses <u>si</u>on) and when the base word has an s at the point where the base word is changed (tense, ten <u>si</u>on).

Rule 13. <u>si</u> saying "zh" is on this page to remind us that si is the only common phonogram for the "zh" sound (di vi <u>si̇̈</u>on).

---

ci is used in gracious and facial because the base words, grace and face, have c where the change comes.

In some words no rule governs the choice of ti, si, or ci for the sound "sh" and the spelling must be memorized, as in influential.

It is important that the vowel sound in each of the last syllables of the words on this page be said accurately.

Vĕ n<u>e</u> <u>ti</u>an (ă), im p<u>a</u> <u>ti</u>ent (ĕ), gr<u>a</u> <u>ci̇̇o</u>us (ŭ)

The first s of conscious and conscientious is silent. The ci of associate and of conscientious say "sh" but since there is no vowel except the i of ci in these syllables, the i is sounded. The syllable <u>ci</u> says "sh<u>ĭ</u>." The syllable <u>ce</u> in oceanic says "<u>she</u>."

Is the cie in the word ancient an exception to Rule 9 illustrated on

[See text pp. 103 & 106]

sh is used at the beginning or end of a
base word and at the end of a syllable
but not at the beginning of any syllable

ti	si
na tion	ses sion
im par tial	com pres sion
sub stan tial	dis cus sion
pà la tial[1]	de pres sion
po ten tial	ad mis sion
pa tience[3]	
tòr ren tial[1]	ten sion (tense)[5]
in fec tious[4]	tran sient (trans it)
in flu en tial	man sion (manse)[5]
am bi tion	
su per sti tious[4]	
con fi den tial	si[2]
col lec tion	
Vé ne tian[1]	vi sion[2]
	di vi sion[2]
	oc ca sion[2]
	ex plo sion[2]

after the first one. ti, si and ci are used to say "sh" at the beginning of a syllable after the first one.

A model of Page Four of the Notebook.

<u>ci</u>

án cient

ra cial

so cial

fi nan cial

{ gla cial

{ gla cier

e lec tri cian   <u>ce</u>

fa cial

gra ci⁴ous   { o cean

phy si cian   { o ce an ic (When

mu si cian   ce is a syllable we

pro fi cien cy   say "she.")

con scious

{ as so ci ate (When ci is a syllable we

{ con sci en tious   say "shi.")

Page 3 in the Notebook? No, because this is ci followed by an e which fact we know from their sounds in this syllable. Unless the phonograms are sounded aloud many rules of spelling do not make sense. It is the failure to combine the sounds with the spelling of English which makes it seem so difficult to learn and makes so many common words seem to be exceptions to the general rules of spelling. This is another good reason why it is important always to teach any new word by writing its spoken sounds.

The use of the sounds of the phonograms permits the pupil to see clearly the relationship between the spoken word, the writing of the word and the reading of it.

After every lesson in the writing of the notebook, each child's writing must be checked by the teacher. She must make sure that the next time he reads from his notebook, he is not seeing errors. One way to do this is to collect the open books from each row and place them in stacks on the teacher's desk. While the class reads silently or perhaps does an arithmetic lesson, one child after the other comes to the teacher who checks for errors, erases each one and has the child make the corrections. If ever time does not permit, the teacher may have to, in out-of-school time, make the corrections herself. The child must *not* see errors in his book.

Notes to the Teacher about Page Five

This page shows when another final consonant is added when endings beginning with a vowel are added to base words.

Rule 14. Words of one syllable (like hop), ending in one consonant, which have only one vowel before this last consonant, require that we add another consonant like the last one before adding an ending that begins with a vowel.

The order of dictating the words on Page 5 is important. The base words on the left-hand page are dictated first. Then dictate the endings which begin with a vowel and discuss how we add the appropriate endings to the base words. (Reasoning is required to use **Rules 14, 15 and 16.**)

Now dictate the second column on the left-hand page. The children should understand that they are using Rule 14 as they write. A quite different intellectual process is required in writing two consonants in base words, such as the two l's of village or the two t's of battle.

The child must learn that he writes the second p in "hopped" to preserve the vowel sound of the base word hop ($\breve{o}$). If the second p is not added the word is hop$\overset{3}{\underline{e}}$d. Its base word is hope as shown on Page 6.

Writ is the archaic past tense of write. We still use "writ" as a noun. Explaining this can help to show why we say "writ ten."

Check to see that the child understands Rule 14. Ask, "How do you add the ending ment to ship?" The child's answer should be, "We do not add another p to ship because ment is not one of the endings which require it. ment begins with a consonant, not a vowel."

Ask, "How do we add '$\overset{3}{\underline{e}}$d' to talk?" The child should reply, "We do not write a second k since this base word ends in two consonants, not just one."

Ask, "How do we add 'er' to red?" The child replies, "We write a second 'd' since red has one syllable, one consonant at the end, one

[See text pp. 107 & 110]

Words of one syllable, ending in one consonant, which have only one vowel before this last consonant (like hop), require that we add another consonant like the last one before adding an ending that begins with a vowel.

hop	hop ping hopped[3]
run	run ning
stop	stopped[3] stop page
red	red dish
hot	hot test
mud	mud dy
flat	flat ten
drug	drug gist
ship	shipped[3] ship per
writ	writ ten

	ing	ice	ous[4]
	er	ish	ist
Endings which	3ed	age	i ble[4]
begin with a	est	{ ance[3]	{ a ble[4]
vowel	y	{ ant	{ a bly
	al	{ ence[3]	{ an cy
	en	{ ent	{ en cy

Words of two syllables, (like begin, where the second syllable gin is like hop, having one consonant at the end and one vowel before it), also require another consonant before adding an ending which begins with a vowel, if the accent is on the last syllable.

A model of Page Five of the Notebook

be gin′	be gin ning
ad mit′	ad mit tance
ac quit′	ac quit tal
oc cur′	oc cur rence
ex cel′	ex cel ling
trans mit′	trans mit ter
for got′	for got ten
con trol′	con trol la ble
re mit′	re mit ted
en′ ter	en ter ing
prof′ it	prof it a ble
can′ cel	can cel ing
trav′ el	trav el ing

vowel before the last consonant and the ending begins with a vowel." Rule 14 can be called the one, one, one rule.

Rule 15. Words of two syllables, like "begin," where the second syllable gin is like hop, having one consonant at the end and one vowel before it, also require that we write another n before adding an ending that begins with a vowel, if the accent is on the last syllable.

Americans use this rule more consistently than do the English.

Ask the children to clap the rhythm of two-syllable words where the above rule applies as they pronounce them. (Notice that acquit conforms to the rule since the u of qu is a consonant sound.)

Words that have the accent on the first syllable, but otherwise would fit the rule, should be clapped also. We should not write the extra consonant in these words when adding an ending beginning with a vowel:

en′ ter, prof′ it, can′ cel, trav′ el

Notes to the Teacher about Page Six

Rule 16. Words ending with one of the five kinds of silent e's are written without the e when adding an ending that begins with a vowel. (hope—hoping)

Dictate the first column of base words. Next dictate the list of endings that begin with a vowel. Then dictate the endings for writing the words in the second column.

Sometimes we cannot drop the e. Changeable holds the e to let the g say "j," since able begins with a vowel, but not an e, i, or y which would permit g to say "j." (See Rule 3.) Such exceptions can be easily understood by children who know the basic rules about c and g.

Hope is written without the e when "ed" is added. In hopèd the e has two functions. It permits the o to say "ō" as well as forming "ed" as an ending.

The teacher says, "Add the ending ĕd, d, t to hope." The class says, "This ending begins with a vowel. Write hope without the e and add the ending ed." It is still a one-syllable word. The pupils must be well taught to see that these endings are added to base words. They must recognize each base word even when the ending forms a separate syllable and the single vowel in the preceding syllable is not marked (hop ing).

In the ending ior, the i is a consonant saying "y," but it acts as a vowel when this ending is added to behave.

es is an ending which also follows Rule 16 (ros es, charg es).

We write fierce and charge without the e to add the ending es, er or est. This allows us (under Rule 2) to keep the "s" sound of c and the "j" sound of g, even though the e is in the next syllable.

Rules 14, 15 and 16 should be taught and well understood as they are needed even in the first grade. The rules on Pages 5 and 6 along with Pages 1 and 2 of the Notebook are basic for all grades.

A parent or teacher who is under the impression that six-year-olds lack the mental ability to learn, understand and apply such rules will be surprised and delighted to see how quickly they do so, and how keen they are about demonstrating this ability to use reasoning in their work.

Words like hope which end with a silent e are written without the e when an ending beginning with a vowel is added.

hope	hoped hop ing
de sire	de sired de sir ing
nerve	nerv ous
be have	be hav ior
fierce	fierc er fierc est
ease	eas y
come	com ing
change	chang ing
serve	serv ice
re hearse	re hears al
set tle	set tling set tler
write	writ ing writ er
	ing ice ous
	er ish ist
Endings	3ed age i ble
beginning with a	est { ance { a ble
vowel	y { ant { a bly
	al { ence { an cy
	en { ent { en cy

Notes to the Teacher about Page Seven

The single consonants are listed on Page 1 of the Notebook and words containing these sounds are on the phonogram cards. The single vowels (with words to prove their sounds) are also on Page 1 of the Notebook.

Page 2 of the Notebook gives five spellings of the sound "er" and a sentence showing all five, which the children learned. (Her first nurse works early.)

The phonograms on this page are dictated and the pupils write in their notebooks. They are numbered 32 through 70 on the phonogram cards. All the seventy phonograms are now in the Notebook and thus readily available at all times for both teacher and pupils.

The following examples of the sounds of these phonograms in words are for the teacher only. The words should not be taught to the pupil because he should not associate these phonograms with any special words. He is to know them, and their sounds, when he writes or sees them in any word.

The teacher can use pages 113 and 116–118 to learn these phonograms. Say only the underlined phonogram in each word.

sh   (di<u>sh</u>)

ee   (s<u>ee</u>)

th   (<u>th</u>in, <u>th</u>is)

[**ay**   (d<u>ay</u>) Used at the end of a word rather than ai.

[**ai**   (p<u>ai</u>nt) Never used at the end of a word.

[**ow**   (n<u>ow</u>, l<u>ow</u> "ō")

[**ou**   (r<u>ou</u>nd "ow," f<u>ou</u>r "ō," y<u>ou</u> "ōō," c<u>ou</u>n try "ŭ")

[**oy**   (b<u>oy</u>) Used at the end of a word rather than oi.

[**oi**   (p<u>oi</u>nt) Never used at the end of a word.

[**aw**   (l<u>aw</u>)

[**au**   (f<u>au</u>lt)

Additional Common Phonograms. The number preceding a phonogram tells how many sounds it has.

sh	3 oo
ee	
2 th	3 ch
{ ay { ai	ng
	3 ea
{ 2 ow { 4 ou	ar
	ck
{ oy { oi	3 ed
{ aw { au	or
	wh
{ 2 ew { 2 ui	oo

3 ey	$\begin{cases} \text{ti} \\ 2\text{ si} \\ \text{ci} \end{cases}$
3 ei	
3 ie	

igh		
eigh		$\begin{cases} \underline{\text{tho}ugh}^2 \\ \underline{\text{thro}ugh}^2 \\ \underline{\text{r}ough}^3 \\ \underline{\text{c}ough}^4 \\ \underline{\text{th}ough}t^5 \\ \underline{\text{b}ough}^6 \end{cases}$
$\begin{cases} \text{kn} \\ \text{gn} \end{cases}$	6 ough	
wr		

ph	

dge	For	$\begin{cases} \text{eu} \\ \text{pn} \\ \text{rh} \\ \text{qu}^2 \\ \text{x}^2 \end{cases}$	$\underline{\text{Eu}}\text{ rope}$
	Grade 4		$\underline{\text{pneu}}\text{ mo ni à}^3$
oe	and above,		$\underline{\text{rh}i}\text{ noc er os}$
gh	or as needed		$\text{mos }\underline{qui}^2\text{ to}$
			$\underline{xy}^2\text{ lo }\underline{phone}$

> **ew**   (gr<u>ew</u> "o͞o," n<u>e̎w</u> "ū")
> **ui**   (fr<u>ui</u>t "o͞o," s<u>u̎i</u>t "ū")

oo   (b<u>oo</u>t "o͞o," f<u>o̎o</u>t "ŏo," fl<u>o̽o</u>r "ō")
ch   (mu<u>ch</u>, s<u>c̎h</u>ool "k," <u>c̽h</u>iv al ry "sh")

ng   (ra<u>ng</u>)
ea   (<u>ea</u>st "ē," h<u>e̎a</u>d "ĕ," br<u>e̽a</u>k "ā")
ar   (f<u>ar</u>)
ck   (ne<u>ck</u> "k") Used only after a single vowel which says ă, ĕ,
          ĭ, ŏ, or ŭ.
ed   (grad <u>ed</u>, love<u>e̎d</u> "d," wrecke<u>e̽d</u> "t")

or   (<u>or</u>)
wh   (<u>wh</u>en)

oa   (b<u>oa</u>t "ō')

The beginner must know the above phonograms as well as the single-letter phonograms before writing the words from the Extended Ayres List. He must know all 70 phonograms to write the words beginning with Section I.

ey   (<u>t̎h</u>ey "ā," k<u>e̎y</u> "ē," val l<u>e̽y</u> "ĭ")

ei   (con c<u>ei</u>t "ē," v<u>e̎i</u>l "ā," for f<u>e̽i</u>t "ĭ")
ie   (f<u>ie</u>ld "ē," p<u>i̎e</u> "ī," lil i<u>ḙs̎</u> "ĭ")

igh   (s<u>igh</u> "ī")
eigh   (w<u>eigh</u> "ā")

> **kn**   (<u>kn</u>ot "n") Used only at the beginning of a base word.
> **gn**   (<u>gn</u>at "n")

wr   (<u>wr</u>ite "r")

ph   (p<u>h</u>an tom "f")

dge   (bri<u>dge</u> "j") May be used only after a single vowel which says ă, ĕ, ĭ, ŏ, ŭ.

oe   (t<u>oe</u> "ō")

gh   (<u>gh</u>ost "g") This phonogram saying "g" is used only at the beginning of a syllable. If i, ei, ou, au, ai come before it, its sound is "f" or it has no sound. igh, eigh, ough, augh and aigh are taught as single phonograms. The last two are seldom used and are not on the phonogram cards. Teach them when a word requires them.

ti   (n<u>a</u> <u>ti</u>on "sh") (See Page 4 in the Notebook.)

si   (ses <u>si</u>on "sh," vi <u>si</u>on "zh")

ci   (f<u>a</u> <u>ci</u>al "sh")

ough   <u>th</u>ough "ō"
  <u>th</u>rou<u>gh</u> "o͞o"
  rou<u>gh</u> "ŭf"
  cou<u>gh</u> "ŏf"
  thou<u>gh</u>t "aw"
  bou<u>gh</u> "ow"

Three of the following phonograms are not listed on the seventy phonogram cards. They are to be taught in Grade IV and above. They are introduced separately at an earlier time as they are needed.

eu   (<u>Eu</u> rop<u>e</u> "ū")

pn   (<u>pneu</u> m<u>o</u> ni <u>a</u> "n") kn, gn, pn are alike in sound.

rh   (r̲h̲i̲ noc e̲r̲ os "r")

q̽u   (mos q̲u̲i̲ to̲ "k") Spanish i says "ē"

x   (x̽y̲ lo̲ p̲h̲o̲n̲e̲ "z")

Spelling Rules

For convenient reference the sixteen rules given in the Teacher's Notes for the first seven pages of the Notebook are listed below. Additional rules are appended and numbered for reference.

Almost no spelling rule is absolute. It is well to make this clear and to say that we shall be on the lookout for words that do not conform to the rules. In the first fifteen hundred words used most often, less than 7 per cent have parts which do not agree with the sounds on the phonogram cards or with these rules of spelling. All these rules hold true often enough to be very helpful. Pupils "discover" words to which the rules do not apply and learn why they do not, if a reason can be found. In that way the words make an impression not quickly forgotten. Finding the word soccer in which we drop the sound of the second c, or façade where c says "s" and is not followed by e, i or y are examples. An unabridged dictionary becomes a fascinating source of information for third-graders and older students about the words of our language.

Page One of the Notebook shows the following seven rules.

Rule 1. q is always written with two letters, qu, when we say "kw." The u is not considered a vowel here.

Rule 2. When c by itself has a sound (not part of a two-letter phonogram) it always says "s" if followed by e, i, or y (cent, city, cyclone). If not followed by one of these letters its sound is "k" (cat, claw, cyclone). This is true in spelling and in reading.

Rule 3. When g has a sound by itself it can say "j" only when followed by e, i, or y. When followed by any other letter it says "g." (Get, girl and give show that e and i following g do not always make the g say "j." In spelling, if g is used to say "j" it must be followed by e, i, or y (pigeon, religious, energy).

Rule 4. Vowels a, e, o, u usually say "ā," "ē," "ō," "ū" at the end of a syllable. This is one of but three ways a vowel may say "ā," "ē," "ī," "ō," or "ū.

Rule 5. i and y can say "ī" at the end of a syllable but usually they say "ĭ." This is shown at the end of the second syllable of both Indĭan and babȳ.

Rule 6. y, not i, is used at the end of an English word. (Taxi is short for taxicab and macaroni is an Italian word. Words like these should be explained when they are met.)

Rule 7. There are five kinds of silent final e's. These five silent e's are indicated by special markings in this book, as shown on page 94. The notes to teachers for this page explain them (see page 96).

Page Two of the Notebook shows five phonograms that say "er."

Rule 8. or may say "er" when w comes before the or, as in work.

Page Three of the Notebook explains Rule 9.

Rule 9. After c we use ei.

If we say "ā" we can use ei (never ie). In the list of exceptions we use ei. In all other words that contain ie or ei we use ie.

Page Four of the Notebook explains the following four rules.

Rule 10. sh may be used at the beginning or end of a base word and at the end of a syllable (she, finish) but except in the ending ship (friendship, worship) not at the beginning of a syllable after the first one.

Rule 11. ti, si, ci are the spellings most frequently used to say "sh" at the beginning of a second or subsequent syllable in a base word.

Rule 12. si is used to say "sh" when the syllable before it ends in an s (ses sion) and when the base word has an s where the base word changes (tense, ten sion).

Rule 13. si (not ti or ci) can also say "zh," as in vision.

Page Five of the Notebook shows the next two rules.

Rule 14. Words of one syllable (like hop) ending in one consonant, which have only one vowel before this last consonant, need
another consonant before adding an ending that begins with a
vowel. (Rule 14 does not apply to words ending in x which has two
sounds, "ks": box ing, ox en).

Rule 15. Words of two syllables, like begin, where the second syllable gin is like hop, having one consonant at the end and one vowel
before it, also need another consonant before adding an ending that
begins with a vowel, *if* the accent is on the last syllable. (Americans
have used this rule more consistently than have the English.)

Page Six of the Notebook shows Rule 16.

Rule 16. Words ending with one of the five kinds of silent e's are
written without the e when adding an ending that begins with a
vowel. (When the ending begins with a vowel which is not e, i, or y
the silent e is retained so that g can say "j" as in changeable, or so the
c can say "s" as in noticeable. Rules 2 and 3 explain this.)

Additional Rules

Rule 17. In English we often double l, f, s following a single
vowel at the end of a word of one syllable as in will, off, glass, roll.
Pupils must learn these and then they must learn words like recess,
distaff, egg and add, when they meet them.

Rule 18. Base words do not end with the letter a saying "ā" (except for the article a). ay is used most often.

Rule 19. The i and o vowels *may* say "ī" and "ō" if followed by
two consonants (find, old).

Rule 20. s never follows x. There is an s sound in x, "ks." Unless a
c followed by e, i, or y can be used there cannot be a second "s"
sound (ex cept, but ex pect).

Rule 21. All, written alone, has double l, but written with another syllable only one l is written (al so, al most).

Rule 22. When till and full are added to another syllable we write one l (until, beautiful).

Rule 23. dge may be used *only* after a single vowel which says ă, ĕ, ĭ, ŏ, or ŭ (badge, ledge, bridge, lodge, budge).

Rule 24. When adding an ending to a word that ends with y that has a sound alone, change the y to i unless the ending is ing: carry is changed to carried and carries but in carrying we keep the y. In English we almost never have an i follow i. In the words played or boys, we do not change the y since it is ay and oy, and not y alone for the sound.

Rule 25. ck may be used only after a single vowel which says ă, ĕ, ĭ, ŏ, or ŭ.

Rule 26. Words which are the individual names or titles of people, of places, of books, of days and months, etc., are capitalized (Mary, Honolulu, Amazon River, Bible, Monday, July).

Rule 27. z (never s) is used to say "z" at the beginning of a base word (zoo).

Rule 28. ed says "d" or "t" as the past-tense ending of any base word which does not end in the sound "d" or "t" (liv<u>ĕd</u>, jump<u>ĕd</u>). If a base word ends in the sound "d" or "t," adding ed makes another syllable which says "ĕd" (sid <u>ed</u>, part <u>ed</u>).

Rule 29. Double consonants within base words of more than one syllable should both be sounded for spelling. In writing little, the pupil says "lit" and writes lit, says "tle" and writes tle. In the rhythm of speech the second t drops out. We say "lit'le." In all such words the consonant is sounded *in the accented syllable*. In accept, both c's are sounded in speech because each c has a different sound, but the word account follows the rule. We say "ă count'." This rule is very important for the teacher to know so that in dictating words she says all such words accurately. With primary children it is best not to talk about this rule. Just make sure they say in reading: "lit'le, ă count', ŏ cur', ĕ fect', ă rive', of' i cer." It is necessary when writing that all students of whatever age pronounce both the consonants to get the spelling correct. Spelling is more difficult than is reading.

CHAPTER V

TEACHING SPELLING BY USING THE PHONOGRAMS AND THE RULES

THE APPLICATION of the phonograms and the spelling rules to learn to spell words is the method which unites the spoken sounds of English words to their written forms. This is taught by analyzing 1700 words which are listed in the order of their frequency of use in the language. They include practically every pattern of English spelling. Seven hundred eighty of these (to the end of Section N, page 190) are taught by mid-April in the first grade.

The words are taught by the pupils' writing from the teacher's dictation only. She teaches them to use the phonograms and the rules of spelling which apply in each word. They do not see the word until they and the teacher have written it.

The dictionary is the standard for spelling and for the meanings of words.

In pronouncing each syllable before he writes it the pupil is taught to stress the vowel sound wherever possible in order to be in agreement with the spelling. In normal speaking or reading, the rhythm of speech and sentence accent, as well as word accent, reduces very naturally many unstressed vowels. The dictionary states that a monosyllable such as the word do (or one syllable of a longer word) when pronounced alone always stresses the vowel. This conforms to the spelling but sometimes differs slightly from the unaccented pronun-

122

ciation when it is spoken in context. This stressing of vowel sounds makes spelling more phonetic and easy to learn. Dictionaries explain the variations in pronouncing words in different contexts and uses.

The teacher dictates the words in the order given in the list. They are not given in categories. She says the *whole* word as spoken in *normal conversation* (not by syllables). She then gives a meaningful sentence containing the word. This develops the habit of mind needed for writing a sentence.

Her sentences can restate useful facts such as how the children should sit, hold the pencil or form letters, facts about how the language works, etc. She can tell the class how good they are at reasoning, studying, playing, and can insert philosophical ideas about learning. They need not be dull, unimaginative sentences, but they should be short and models of good English. They serve as standards for the type of sentences she wants from the pupils when their turn comes to use a word in a sentence—at first orally. In two weeks the beginner will have gotten to Section H and each child can begin writing his own sentences. The subject for their separate sentences should be a noun, not a pronoun, except for I, which should be used infrequently. Two or three sentences a day are sufficient for first grade.

The class in unison says aloud the first phonogram of a one-syllable word and writes it. As each one writes that sound, he says aloud the next one and writes it until the word is finished. For words of more than one syllable the class says the first syllable aloud and starts to write it. Before finishing it, they say aloud the next syllable, write it and so on until the word is finished. The saying aloud should be distinct but done softly by each child. This way the sounds flow to form the word. After each word is written the class reads it aloud as each pupil checks what he has written.

Teach the process of reading as contrasted with the process of writing. In writing, *saying* the sounds of a phonogram or syllable precedes the writing of it to permit the *mind* to *direct* the *hand* in forming the correct phonogram or phonograms. In reading, the eyes must *see first* the phonograms in proper sequence, then take these to the *mind* to interpret them before saying the word. The eyes must be on what is being read.

Do not use nonsense syllables. Everything written and read should be sensible so that pupils come to expect words they write and those they read to make sense to them.

The pupils do *not* repeat the word the teacher says. They know the word from her saying of it. Their job is to give immediately the first sound, or first syllable. This is the way they will write words they say to themselves as they write their own sentences.

The *names* of the letters are *not* said unless the sound and the name is the same. (The few exceptions are noted.) This permits each child to write about as fast as he can speak distinctly and it unites writing (spelling) with speech and reading. It is one of the most valuable parts of all the techniques which Dr. Orton taught me.

Program for Teaching Extended Ayres List to Beginners through the Second Grade

No child should be asked to use the tools of a written language until his teacher has taught them to him. In the first few years of life he has learned to use or understand at least 3000 words. This is a far more complicated skill than learning to write and read them. Make this fact clear on the first day of school. There are only forty-five sounds and seventy phonograms for writing them. Begin at once to teach the class to say all the sounds and to write the first fifty-four phonograms (pages 68–78 and 34–50). First-graders require three weeks, fifteen days, for this if only four new phonograms are taught each day. Schedule three hours each day divided into suitable periods, including time for those who need more attention. Teach the parents enough so that they can enjoy helping their children at home and especially those children who need extra help.

Writing the words of the Extended Ayres List is begun by beginners after they have learned the sounds with the writing of the manuscript alphabet (pages 68–78) and the rest of the fifty-four phonograms. Knowledge of these phonograms is tested by having the teacher dictate the sound or sounds of each phonogram (without the children seeing the phonogram card) and having them write the phonogram.

They must know how to write the numbers from 0 to 9 (pages 80–82).

Teach the capital letters as needed to write the name of each child. Teach the other capitals, along with the reasons for them, when needed.

By October 1 first-graders should begin writing the words in Sections A–H. Teach them at least thirty words a week so that by November 1 they reach Section I, when they will begin to read aloud from their first book. Schedule a daily reading lesson at this time. Let each child who can read aloud to the class.

Continue teaching thirty or more words a week so that 780 words to Section O (page 190) are taught in the twenty-four weeks before mid-April.

Give the first fifteen words of a Morrison-McCall Spelling Scale Test in December. A score of 2.6 can be made if the pupils know the words taught them to date. This much is needed for first graders to write and read with accuracy and independence on their grade level. The top score can be 3.1 if all fifteen words are correct. In the January test dictate twenty-five words so as to test the children with facility. In subsequent monthly tests go far enough so as to place no limit on the scores the children with facility can make. (see page 128).

Since 1964 the Stanford Achievement battery has included a first-grade spelling test, showing that many educators now know that early spelling is a necessary skill for accurate reading and writing. Their top score is 3.4. Some first graders can make 7.0 scores.

Second graders beginning this method follow the first-grade program. Note the errors in formation of letters and knowledge of phonograms made on the first Morrison-McCall Spelling Test. These will indicate how fast the pace can be in teaching for the first several weeks. If spelling scores are not third-grade, spend three hours a day teaching as outlined above for beginners.

Notebooks for First Grade and Younger and for Second Grade

First-grade and younger pupils first write the first thirty words of the Extended Ayres List in Sections A–H, on separate sheets having ⅜-inch spaces between the lines. This gives them time to attain good writing skills. Divide each sheet for two columns of words by putting a vertical crease down the middle. No margins are required for writing spelling words.

Dictate these words again so that each pupil can write them neatly in his own spelling notebook beginning on its *first* page. The new words of each new lesson should then be put directly in his notebook.

A *sewn* composition book about 8 inches by 7 inches with about fifty pages, each with twelve lines ⅜ inches apart, and stiff covers is needed. (A thicker book raises the child's arm too high.) This notebook becomes each first-grader's prized *spelling* book of 780 words by mid-April. All words written in the notebooks should be divided into syllables, and show all the markings (see pages 130–131).

Number the notebook pages and dictate ten words to be put in each column (a line is drawn down the center of each page) so that the books will be alike and can be used for class assignments.* Have the words read across the line as well as down the column so as to change their order. This practice is needed until they are read easily enough to require no attention when they are met in reading stories.

* Notebooks with lines ⅜ inches apart and pads of paper are available from

Spalding Education Foundation
15410 N. 67th Ave., Suite 8,
Glendale, AZ 85306

Requirements before Teaching Extended Ayres List to Third-grade and Older Students, including Adults

The Extended Ayres List is begun by those in Grade 3 or older students after they have learned to say and write all the seventy phonograms in manuscript writing (pages 58–79) and then in cursive writing (pages 83–88). The test of the knowledge of these phonograms is the same as for first-grade beginners. The writing of numbers is also required (pages 80–82).

Teaching Program for Third-grade and Older Students

A *sewn* (not ring-type) hard-cover composition book, 7¾ inches by 10 inches, with fifty sheets, each with about twenty lines ruled with ⅜-inch spacing, is required for each student.

On the first page of his notebook each student writes from dictation all of Page 1 of the Notebook (see page 94). The notes to the teacher about this are on the adjoining pages.

Next dictate the top line of Page 2 of the Notebook (pages 98–99). Five columns are needed for this. Divide the top line of the *back* of Page 1, a single sheet, into three equal parts and draw two lines from the top line to the bottom of the page so as to have three columns. Crease the next page down the center. This gives the five columns on the double page, Page 2 of the Notebook. Dictate only the sentence on the top line. Have each word centered on each column. Next turn the page and dictate the four headings for the double page, Page 3 of the Notebook. A crease down the center of each uncreased sheet provides the two columns necessary on each page to be written on, in the rest of the notebook. Turn the page and center on the top line in each of the first three columns the phonograms given on Page 4 of the Notebook. Center ce halfway down the fourth column. (ce says "sh" but is not used often.) On the double page, Page 5 of the Notebook, dictate the word hop to be put in the first column, and in the third column dictate the word begin. All words written alone in this spelling book are written in syllables.

On the double page, Page 6 of the Notebook, dictate hope, which is to be written in the center of the first column on the top line. Leave the next three columns blank.

Use the next double page for Page 7 (pages 114, 115) and dictate the phonograms through ough in the four columns (cards 32 through 70). See notes to teachers on pages 113–118.

The last five phonograms on Page 7 and the rest of the words for Pages 2 through 6 will be filled in as they are needed.

In their notebooks the children of third grade and above now have all the seventy phonograms to which they can readily refer. The single letters and the final silent e's are on Page 1 and the five er's are on Page 2.

Sections A to H of the Extended Ayres List (page 133) can be started in the middle of the Notebook, where the stitching makes it open easily. The words through Section N are taught to the first-graders. Older students who are starting on this method need to be taught these words by exactly the same techniques as the beginners, but they should progress much more rapidly after a few days of initial teaching.

Written Spelling Tests

The Morrison-McCall Spelling Scale* is a booklet of eight standardized, fifty-word tests of equal difficulty. They were selected from the Extended Ayres List of 1700 words, which begins in this book on page 132. These words also appear in the 5000 most commonly used words as reported in Thorndike's Word Book.

The grade scores for each test range from Grade 1.0 to Grade 13, first-year college. Many fourth-, fifth- and sixth-graders make this top score when they have been taught the words in this book.

Give one of these tests during the first day of school to all second-graders and older students before beginning the teaching from the Extended Ayres List. This will tell how well students spell without any review. These tests put a high ceiling on the score the top student can make, and the poor student shows where in the list you

*Booklets from Spalding Education Foundation, 15410 N. 67th Ave., Suite 8, Glendale, Arizona 85306.

need to go to develop his ability in written spelling. Spelling scores are usually lower than reading scores in the United States. Spelling is harder than reading because in spelling all the knowledge must come from the mind. Written spelling, taught skillfully and logically and far enough, can upgrade all children's speech and reading, two basic elements for education.

For second-graders, dictate the first thirty-five words. Beyond the second grade, dictate all fifty words. Check each misspelled word but put at the top of each paper the number of words spelled correctly and the grade equivalent. Table 2 on page 4 of the booklet lists the grade equivalents.

Mark on each paper where the first word has been misspelled. The Extended Ayres List is divided into sections. The first five words in each of these tests were taken from Sections A to H. Words 7 and 8 are from Section H, 9 and 10 from I, 11 and 12 from J, 13 and 14 from K, 15 and 16 from L, 17, 18 from M, 19, 20 from N, 21 23 from O, 24, 25 from P, 26, 27 from Q, 28–31 from R, 31, 32 from S, 33–35 from T, 36, 37 from U, 38–40 from V, 41, 42 from W, 43, 44 from X, 45, 46 from Y and 47–50 from Section Z.

Put the section letter at the first misspelled word. If a student misses but a few words after this first word, mark the place where he begins missing many words. Note the kinds of errors found on each paper, reversals, poor letter formation, mistakes in phonograms or patterns of English. Spelling scores should be at least one year above the grade placement for each child. He can then do creditable work at his grade level and with further study soon at a higher level.

Do not show the scored paper to any student, and teach the missed words along with all the words in the sections from which they came. These tests are then valid for many years.

A different test should be given at the same time each month. Keep a class record of the students' scores. This monthly record measures the effectiveness of the teaching and shows the teacher what is needed for each child's advancement. Principals who give the tests each month find they can share in the pleasure of seeing students learn.

Markings to Identify Phonogram Sounds in Spelling Notebooks

The following five items explain the simple markings of the words which are used to teach pupils how the rules and phonograms actually work.

1   A vowel is underlined at the end of a syllable when it says ā, ē, ī, ō or ū.

    m<u>e</u>

    <u>o</u> pen

    J<u>u</u> l<u>y</u>

(Spelling Rule 5 states that i and y usually say "ī" at the end of a syllable. Where this is true i and y are not underlined— fam i ly.)

2   Phonograms of two or more letters are underlined.

    <u>th</u>in

    bri<u>dg</u>e

    <u>eigh</u>t

3   Silent letters and phonograms, when their sound is one not given on the phonogram cards, have a double line under them.

    ha<u>l</u>f (We say "haf" but write half.)

    fri<u>e</u>nd (ĕ is not one of the sounds on card 57 for ie.)

The silent e at the end of a base word is one of five different kinds and each kind is marked as shown below. All except the first kind have a number below the base line to show which kind it is. (See the Teacher's Notes for Page 1 of the Notebook.)

    t<u>ime</u>

    hav<u>e</u>₂   blu<u>e</u>₂

    <u>chance</u>₃   <u>charge</u>₃

    lit tl<u>e</u>₄

    <u>are</u>₅

4 Numbers are placed above a phonogram when its sound is not the first sound given on its card. (Except where a line is used under a vowel which says its name at the end of a syllable.)

$\overset{3}{\text{do}}$ $\underset{\rule{0pt}{0pt}}{\text{lo}\overset{2}{\text{w}}}$

$\text{wa}\overset{3\ 2}{\text{s}}$ $\text{y}\underset{\overline{}}{\overset{3}{\text{ou}}}$

$\text{p}\overset{3}{\text{u}}\text{t}$ $\text{c}\underset{\overline{}}{\overset{4}{\text{ou}}}\text{n try}$

          $\underline{\text{thou}\overset{5}{\text{gh}}\text{t}}$

          $\underline{\text{bou}\overset{6}{\text{gh}}}$

5 Some words are bracketed together. In such cases the first word is in the Extended Ayres List. The others have been added to show (1) the base word, or (2) several words with the same peculiarity in spelling, or (3) how some words are said alike but use different phonograms in spelling, or (4) contrast in the sounds of two words that might easily be confused.

Instructions for Teaching Spelling of Words of the Extended Ayres List

These words are presented orally. The pupils do not see them until they and the teacher write them.

The teacher says the first word me. She gives a sentence containing me. The word is not unfamiliar. The meaning is clear. The only problem is how to write it. The class says the sound of the first phonogram they hear in the word, "m." As they and the teacher start the writing of m they say "ē." The teacher says, "We write the letter which says ĕ, ē." They underline the e and the teacher points out that a, e, o, u usually says "ā," "ē," "ō," "ū" at the end of a syllable (Rule 4). The pupils then read me aloud as a word. Be sure their eyes are on the word as they read it. They can then prove it says me by sounding the two phonograms as they did for writing it.

The teacher then dictates the word do and gives a sentence containing do. The pupils say "d" and before finishing the writing of d they say "ōō." The teacher says, "We write the letter which says ŏ, ō, ōō." They write o and put a 3 exactly above it because we say its third sound. They then read "dŏ."

The teacher then dictates the next word and. In unison the class says ă. The teacher says, "We write the letter which says ă, ā, ah." She and the pupils write a. Before finishing the writing of a they say "n" and start writing n, say "d" and write d. The word and needs no markings because ă is the first sound of its phonogram and "n" and "d" have but one sound. Follow the same procedure for teaching all words in the Extended Ayres List.

Never confuse by discussing any other phonogram which *might* give the same sound in a given word. Keep to the facts about each word being studied. The teacher shares her knowledge of the exact phonograms which the dictionary shows for writing each word. The dictionary is referred to as the standard for spelling.

Most of the first 700 words in the Extended Ayres List are in the spoken or understood vocabulary of six-year-old children. If not, they are so basic they must be taught.

After each word is written the pupils read it. After all the words of the lesson are written oral sentences containing each word should be given by the beginning children.

Some critics of phonics assume that if the sounds are taught the meaning of individual words is overlooked. It is quite the opposite with this method which emphasizes meaning with the writing of each word. Before the beginner finishes learning the words in Sections A to H (just as in the above examples of me, do, and) he knows enough words to write his own original sentences to show the meaning of each new word. He should write two or three good sentences each day.

A spelling rule (pages 118–121) is taught when a word illustrates it. In this way the children come to understand a rule and use it, instead of having a mere parroted memorizing of it—a most important difference.

Spelling Words of the Extended Ayres List
Study the above techniques and the five numbered explanations of underline and number markings and brackets on pages 129–130. The

twenty-nine rules are on pages 118–121. Follow instructions about pupils' notebooks on pages 125–127.

Use detailed teaching instructions for kindergarten, pre-school and each of the grades as given in Chapter VI.

Sections A through G

me	**Rule 4** (e says "ē" at the end of a syllable.)
do³	The third sound on the phonogram card for o is "ōō".
and	
go	**Rule 4** (o says "ō" at the end of a syllable.)
at	
on	
a	**Rule 4** (a may say "ā" because it ends the syllable. In speech and reading the accent is almost never on the article a. Say "ā" but do not hold it in saying a man, a house, etc.
it	
is²	(s says "z," the second sound on its card.)

she

Rule 4 (It takes two letters to write the sound "sh.")

can

(We use the short "c," not the tall "k," at the beginning of all common words when the next letter is not an e, i, or y.)

see

(We use ee to write "ē" in see. When children are writing words for the first time the teacher tells them which phonogram the dictionary uses where there are several possibilities.)

run

the

Rule 4 (Write the 2 at the top between the letters th.)

in

so

Rule 4

no

Rule 4

now

(There are two cards for the sound "ow." We use ow here since English words should not end with u.)

man

ten

Also dictate tan, tin, ton. In ten we use the phonogram "ĕ, ē," in tan "ă, ā, ah," in tin "ĭ, ī" and in ton "ŏ, ō, ōō." Teach the importance of using the right vowel to express the intended meaning.

bed

top

he̲   **Rule 4**

yo̲u̲³   (The third sound on the card for ou is "o͞o." You and thou are two of the few words that end with ou. y at the beginning of a word is always the consonant y. This is important for reading only, since in translating sound there is but one phonogram given for the consonant "y.")

will   **Rule 17** (We often double l, f, s, following a single vowel at the end of one-syllable words.)

we̲   **Rule 4**

an

my̲   (English words do not end with i. We use y which has the sounds of i and we treat it as an i.)

up

last   (We use s, not c, since Rule 2 shows c would say "k" here.)

not

us

am

goo̲d²   (The second sound for oo is "o͝o.")

Dictate the five kinds of silent e's found on page 1 of the Notebook (pages 94 and 96).

A bracket is set before two or more words. It does not touch them and is made without lifting the pencil. Start with a tiny horizontal line at the height halfway between the top line and the line on which the first word sits. Continue with a straight down line and end with a tiny line just below and parallel to the base line of the last word.

time

have₌₂   blue₌₂

chance₌₃   charge₌₃

lit tle₌₄

are₌₅ (no job e)

lit tle₌₄   The pupils now can say "lit" and write it, then "tle" and write it. In the spelling notebooks words are written in syllables. (In writing sentences of course, they cannot be divided.)
Using the two hands to give the kinesthetic feel of the two syllables helps here. (Rule 29) See pages 90, 91.

a go   **Rule 4** (Child says "ā" and writes it, then "go" and writes it.)

old   **Rule 19** (i or o may say ī or ō if followed by two consonants.) 2 above o is not necessary. Rule 19 explains the sound, and ŏld is not a word.

bad

red

of
=

(We say "v" but write "f." Both must be learned. Put two lines under f. They indicate here that the sound we write for spelling is different from the sound in speech.)

be

Rule 4

but

²this

³all

The teacher tells that we use the letter that says, "ă, ā, ah" when the children give the first sound of all.

Rule 17 (The third sound of a is "ah" on its phonogram card.)

³your

³you

(you is the base word of your.)

out

In the first presentation the teacher shows the ou card (which says "ow, ō, ōo, ŭ") to write the first sound of out.

time

No. 1 on Page 1 of the Notebook. We put the silent e on so the i can say "ī." Without the e the word would be Tim. However, we did not make time from Tim.

The pupils have now met the three usual ways for a vowel to say ā, ē, ī, ō, or ū:

1　by ending the syllable (m<u>e</u>)
2　by being followed by a consonant and a silent e (t<u>ime</u>)
3　by having two consonants follow it (old, find)

It follows that the o of of should say ŏ, the u of but should say ŭ, etc.

may　　　　　　　　　(At the end of a base word we often use ay to say "ā", never a alone, except in the article a.)

in to

him

to day

look　　　　　　　　The teacher tells that we use the card that says "ōo, ŏo, ō" to say "ŏo" in look.
　　　　　　　　　　　Rule 25　(We could not use ck at the end.)

did

like　　　　　　　　Page 1 of the Notebook. We need the silent e so the i can say "ī." (We must use k, not c, to say "k.")

six

boy　　　　　　　　**Rule 6** shows why we would not use oi here.

book

by　　　　　　　　y says ī. It is treated as an i.

have

Refer to the five kinds of silent e now in the Notebook. The a says "ă" but we still need the e. English words do not end with v.

are

Page 1 of the Notebook. This is a silent e with no job. The five kinds of silent final e's (see page 136) are in the children's notebook for ready reference.

had

o ver

Page 2 of the Notebook gives five spellings for "er." This er we use most often. Dictate: Her first nurse works early. The children in kindergarten, first and second grade write it on the top line of their notebooks above where the word over is to be written.

must

make

Page 1 of the Notebook. The e lets the a say "ā." We could not use c to say "k" because we need the e so the a can say "ā" and the e would make a c say "s."

mace

school

(The second sound of ch is "k.") It takes four phonograms to write school.

street

It takes five phonograms to write street.

say

come

Page 1 of the Notebook. This silent e has no job.

hand

ri<u>ng</u>   Be sure each pupil says ng correctly.

li<u>ve</u>   (Page 1 of the Notebook) The e lets the i say "ī."

live   The i says "ĭ" in live but we need the silent e since no word may end with v. Always start from the beginning of a word to find the spelling rule which applies.

kill   **Rule 17** (We use c at the beginning of common words when we can. Here we cannot for it would say "s.")

l<u>ate</u>   The e lets the a say "ā."

let

big   Dictate bag, beg, bog, bug also.

mo<u>th</u> <u>er</u>   (Page 2 of the Notebook gives five spellings of the sound "er." We use er more often than the other four. The dictionary says we say "ŭ" instead of "ŏ." The overtone "ŏ" can be said in saying individual syllables for spelling, and speech becomes more precise.

thr<u>ee</u>

land

cold   **Rule 19**

hot

hat

child   **Rule 19**

ice   The e lets the i say "ī."
                              Rule 2 is secondary here.

play

sea   ee and ea (each saying "ē") show that the words
see   have different meanings.

86 words are now in the children's notebooks. For beginners this has taken three weeks if 30 words are studied each week.

Grade 1 children can begin at Section H to write their own original sentences. A separate period should be scheduled for this. At first have a child give a sentence orally and then have him write it on the board. Discuss the need for a capital at the beginning and a period or question mark at the end. Train him to ask for help in writing a word of which he is not sure. He gives the sounds and the teacher gives the sound or sounds of the phonogram he does not know. The class listens. Then have each child choose a word from the spelling lesson and write either on paper or on the board his own sentence. Edit those on the board so as to constantly teach the techniques of writing a sentence with good content.

Section H

Start each section in the notebooks in a new column with the section letter centered on the top line of the column.

Do not relax nor shorten the method of presenting the following words. Follow in detail the same procedure in teaching each word as outlined at the beginning of the list.

Dictate to Grade 3 and above all the words on the double page, Page 2, for writing in the front of their notebooks. See pages 97–99.

d<u>ay</u>

<u>ea</u>t

The teacher tells that the dictionary uses the phonogram "ē, ĕ, ā" for the ē sound in eat. The pupils should be able to give this information to the teacher when eat is dictated in subsequent lessons.

sit

lot

b<u>o</u>x

(x = "ks" in sound.) See page 75, for writing x.

b<u>e</u> lo<u>ng</u>

Rule 4

d<u>o͞o</u>r
fl<u>o͞o</u>r

(door and floor are the only words in this list in which oo says "ō." In all other words oo will say "o͞o" "o͝o.")

yes

l<u>o̅w</u>

s<u>o</u>ft

sta<u>nd</u>

<u>ya</u>rd

bri<u>ng</u>

tell   **Rule 17**

five   (The e lets the i say "ī." This is its primary job.)

ball   **Rule 17** (The third sound for a is "ah" as shown on its phonogram card and on Page 1 of the Notebook. This is a slight overtone here for spelling.)

law   (We use aw, not au, at the end of a word since u should not end a word.)

ask   (k, not ck, is used because a consonant sits before. ck can be used only after a single vowel).

just   (We must write j here, for g would say "g" since it is not followed by e, i, or y.)
gust

way

get

home   The e lets the o say "ō."

much

call   **Rule 17**

long

love   The e is needed since no English word may end in v.

th**e̲n**

h**ou̲se**₌₅ — The ou sound in house is from the card ou (which says "ow, ō, o͞o, ŭ"). The e has no job.

y**ea̲r** — (Year has three phonograms.)

t**ŏ**

I̲ — This is one of the few exceptions to Rule 6. The pronoun I is always capitalized. Early printers found the lower-case i looked insignificant as a word.

a**s̓**

send

[**one**

  l**o̲ne**

  a l**o̲ne**] — (Spell one by saying the names of the letters if necessary. We probably once said one as in lone and only which mean one. Since we say "won" the correct spelling must be learned. of and one are the only words in the first 275 words where a sound and its written form are not in agreement.)

ha**s̓**

s**om̲e**₌₅ — The e has no job.

if

h**ow̲**

h**e̲r**

$\overset{2}{\underline{th}}$em

o$\overset{2}{\underline{th}}$ er

b$\underline{a}$ by   (y says "ī." Be sure the children say "ī." To write babies we change the y of baby to i and add es. Rule 24)

well   **Rule 17**

$\underline{a}$ b$\underline{ou}$t

⌈ men

⌊ man

f$\underline{or}$

⌈ ran

⌊ run

w$\overset{3\,2}{a}$s   (The first time was is sounded and written the teacher tells which phonograms to use. The next time the children will tell which phonograms we write.)

$\overset{2}{\underline{th}}$at

hi$\overset{2}{s}$

led

lay   **Rule 18**

ap pl$\underline{\underline{e}}_4$

dog

bre̲a̲d (with superscript 2 over the a)

e̲ats (When s is added to a base word say it with a word or two after it to determine its sound: "eats food," "dog̲s bark.")

fo̲o̲d

(This is the point of accomplishment in a first grade with 149 words by November. The class as a whole should now start reading from easy books. See the Appendix and pages 256 to 262.)

Beginners through Grade 2 should now learn the rest of the seventy phonograms (cards 55–70). Teach four each day for four days.

Dictate frequently in varying sequences the sounds of the seventy phonograms (without showing them to the class) and have the pupils write them. They can be done in sets of thirty. Have the class then dictate these sounds to the teacher, who writes the phonograms on the chalkboard as each pupil checks his paper.

Children who cannot write and read (with clear speech) words and single sentences cannot successfully read progressively more difficult books. Therefore give most of the daily three hours available to the spelling lessons so as to reach Section M by February and Section O by mid-April. This permits the books used in the daily reading lessons to be of ever increasing interest and educational content.

Section I

The five kinds of silent e found on Page 1 of the Notebook will no longer have a notation after them. They will be underlined and numbered as they are on Page 1 of the Notebook.

n**ine**

face   (c can be used since we put an e after it. The children must learn to write c in this word. Drill is necessary.)

miss   **Rule 17**

⌈ **ride**

⌊ **rides**²

tree

sick   (ck is used here after a single vowel.)

got

north

white   (wh has no sound but air can be felt on the hand held before the lips. Ask children to blow air out and feel it on their hands. "white" not wite.)

spent

⌈ **foot**²

⌊ **feet**

⌈ **blow**²

⌊ **blows**² ²

block

spri<u>ng</u>

plant

riv <u>er</u>   (The child says "riv" and writes it, if he can,
                          without sounding the individual sounds. Before
                          finishing the writing of riv he says er and writes
                          er.)

cut

so<u>ng</u>

si<u>ng</u>

sa<u>ng</u>

su<u>ng</u>

win <u>ter</u>

st<u>one</u>

fr<u>ee</u>

l<u>ake</u>

l<u>ace</u>

p<u>age</u>

n<u>ice</u>

end

fȁll   Rule 17

went

bac**k**

a way

p**a** p**er**

pu̬t

each

s**oo**n

c**a**m**e**

Sun day   **Rule 26** (Sunday is the name that was given to
                one day. Like a person's name, it must be writ-
                ten with a capital letter. Sunday was named for
                the sun.)

sho̅w

Mon day   **Rule 26** (Monday is the name given to one day
                and must be written with a capital letter. Mon-
                day was named for the moon.)

m**oo**n   (Not capitalized. There are many moons and
                suns.)

yet

We write the letter which says "ŭ, ū, o̅o̅."

find

Rule 19

give
-=2

n<u>ew</u>
2

ew says "ū"

let t<u>er</u>

t<u>ake</u>

Mr. = <u>Mis</u> t<u>er</u>   In Mr. we chose the first and the last letter and put a period at the end. When we leave out letters of a single word and put a period at the end it is an abbreviation. The first letter of a word is always used. The dictionary shows what other letter or letters to use in any abbreviation. Mr. is always written with a man's name (Mr. Brown). Rule 26. lb. = pound. lb. comes from the Latin word libra, a pound in weight. etc. is from two Latin words, et cetera, meaning and others, but an abbreviation of an English word represents only a single word.

af t<u>er</u>

<u>thing</u>

wh<u>a</u>t
3

Be sure children do not say "watt" for "what." Explain both meanings.

<u>than</u>
2

its, his², he**r**	Its is used as we use her or his and, like them, needs no apostrophe. It is not a contraction.
it's = it (i)s²	The apostrophe is used in place of the ĭ of is. When we put two single-syllable words together and leave out a vowel and perhaps other letters, an apostrophe is inserted where letters are omitted. This is a contraction. An apostrophe, like a comma, is a tiny half clock from 12 to 6. It is placed at the height halfway between the size of a short and tall letter.
vér¹ y	The e says "ĕ." Three phonograms are needed to write ver. The y says "ĭ." Rule 5
or	
thank	(We say "thangk" but for spelling say "th," "ă," "n," "k.")
d**ea**r	
west	
sold	Rule 19
told	Rule 19
be**s**t	
form	
fa**r**	
gav**e**	

a like

add   Rule 17

brave

corn

dance₃

din ner

doll   Rule 17

egg   Rule 17

looks

rich

[zoo   Rule 27

  zip

  ze ro

Section J

sev en

for get

hap py   (y says "ĭ.") Rule 29

noon

think

sis ter

cast

card

south

deep

in side

blue₂

post   Rule 19

town

stay

grand

out side

dark

band

game

boat

rest

east

son   Sound ŏ for spelling and precise speech.

sun

help

h<u>ar</u>d

r<u>ace</u>

cov <u>er</u>

f<u>ire</u>   Be sure the children say "r" and do not say "fi̲
                       er." (These words have but one syllable.)
w<u>ire</u>

t<u>ire</u>

<u>age</u>

gold   **Rule 19**

r<u>ea</u>d   (a book)

r<u>ĕa</u>d   (a book)

red

f<u>ine</u>

can not

M<u>ay</u>   **Rule 26**

m<u>ay</u>

l**ine**

left

ship

train

saw

pay

large₃

near

down

why   (Not "wy")

bill

want

girl   (Page 2 in Notebook) See note on p. 139 associated with the word "over."

part

still

pl**ace**

re p**or**t

nev **er**

f**ou**nd

side

kind

life

here

car

word   (Page 2 of the Notebook)

ev **er** y

un d**er**

most   Rule 19

m**ade**

s**ai**d   (Say ā when writing. The base word is say. We
                           say "sĕd" in speaking. Both the writing and the
                           reading must be learned since the two are differ-
say   ent.)

w<u>or</u>k   (Page 2 of the Notebook)

<u>our</u>

m<u>o̲r̲e̲</u>

<u>wh</u>en

from   From has four phonograms.

f<u>or</u>m   Form has three phonograms.

wind   (An i does not have to say ī when followed by two consonants.)

wind²   (the clock) **Rule 19** The 2 over i is necessary to distinguish wind from wind² when not shown in a sentence.

print

<u>ai</u>r

fill   **Rule 17**

<u>a</u> lo<u>ng</u>

lost

n<u>a̲m̲e̲</u>

r<u>oo</u>m

h<u>o̲p̲e̲</u>

s<u>a̲m̲e̲</u>

glad

wit͟h (with 2 over th)

mine

chair

for got

girls (girls with 2, underline under l)   (Page 2 in the Notebook)

hang

meat

mouse (mouse with double underline and 5)

sits

store

sup per   Rule 29

332 words are now in the spelling notebooks, taking the first grade a total of eleven weeks to the middle of December if only thirty words a week were presented.

At this point we should discuss base words and derivatives. Many words are derived from "base" words and it is always important for word meaning, grammar and a grasp of how the language is formed that the base word is taught with each derived word. For example, please is the base word for pleasant, pleasure, displease, etc. It is important also that the children learn that, although many words contain the spellings of shorter words which are not related in meaning—this fact is a mere coincidence which they should ignore. The phonics teaching now being used in many schools classifies rhyming words like ill, will, bill, fill, kill, mill, etc., as word families. This is wrong. They are not families but completely unrelated words.

Section K

Read again the directions for presenting spelling words on the first two pages of Chapter V. The teacher's use of her hands in representing syllables and her fingers in representing the phonograms within a syllable can be of great assistance to the pupil who finds it difficult to learn to write words correctly. See page 91. The class then says these sounds aloud just before they write them in their notebooks. They then dictate the word to the teacher, who writes it on the board so that they can edit what they have already written. Train each pupil to learn well when the teacher first presents a word instead of learning by correcting his mistakes or by drill. Make him responsible from the start. Daily tests will show how well each one does this.

be came

broth er

rain

keep

start

mail

male

fe male

eye (eye)

I

Rule 4 Eye is not phonetic. The drawing gives the spelling and suggests the meaning. Each e represents an eye, and y the nose between. This is the only one in these 1700 spelling words where a picture is helpful to learning the spelling. There are *no* other pictures that help teach the writing of sounds or the writing (spelling) of words. Using pictures hinders the direct use of sounds to or from their symbols.

glass

par ty   y says "ī."

up on

two³
twin
twice
twen ty
be tween

(For spelling say the sounds of the three letters we write. We probably once said "two" sounding the "w" as we still do in twin, twice, twelve, twenty, twain and between, each of which relates to two.)

they²

would

(For writing say "w" "oo²" "l" "d." oo² is an uncommon sound of ou. The l came from will, the present tense of would. We say "woo²d.")

an y

(Sound "ă" as it is written for spelling. We say "ĕ" in normal speech and in reading.)

man y

could

(Sound "c" "oo²" "l" "d" for writing. The present tense is can but the l was inserted to make the analogy with would and should. We say "c$\overset{2}{oo}$d.")

should   (Sound "sh$\overset{2}{oo}$ld" for writing. We say sh$\overset{2}{oo}$d. The l comes from shall.)

cit y

$\overset{2}{on}$ ly   The base word is one saying "one." Normally the e would be retained to let the o say $\bar{o}$ since the ending ly does not begin with a vowel (Rule 16). Explain that this is an exception.

where$_5$ (Not w$\overset{3}{ea}$r)

week

weak

first   (Page 2 in the Notebook)

sent

·cent

mile

seem   (Base word is see)

see

e ven

with out

af ter noon

Fri day   **Rule 26** (Friday was named for Frigga, the wife of Odin, in Norse Myth.)

hour   (For spelling pronounce the "h." Compare meaning with our.)

our

wife

state

Ju ly   **Rule 26**

head

sto ry

o pen

short

la dy   (y says "ī.")

reach

bet ter

wa ter

round

cost

price

be come

class   Rule 17

horse

care

try

move

de lay   Rule 18

pound

be hind   Rule 19

a round

burn   (Page 2 of the Notebook)

camp

bear

bare

clear

clean

spell

poor

fin ish

h<u>ur</u>t

(Page 2 of the Notebook)

m<u>ay</u> b<u>e</u>

(It may be—is the meaning. A word made up of two distinct words is called a compound word.)

<u>a</u> cross

Rule 17

t<u>o</u>³ n<u>igh</u>t

(We write igh, the three-letter "ī.")

ten<u>th</u>

s<u>ir</u>

(Page 2 of the Notebook)

⎡ th²<u>e</u>s²<u>e</u>

⎣ th²<u>o</u>s²<u>e</u>

club

⎡ s<u>ee</u>n

(Base word is see.)

⎣ s<u>ee</u>

fel<u>t</u>

f³<u>u</u>ll

Rule 17

f<u>a</u>il

set

stamp

li<u>gh</u>t

First- and second-grade teachers now teach Page 5 of the Notebook (see page 108 and the notes on page 107) and Page 6 (page 112 and the notes on page 111). The pupils write appropriate words from these pages from dictation on separate sheets, *not* in their notebooks, as the teacher explains and writes on the board.

Third-grade teachers and teachers of all older students now dictate all the words on Pages 5 and 6 of the Notebook. Follow the directions to teachers on pages 107, 110 and 111.

com <u>ing</u> **come**₅	(Page 6 of the Notebook) Come is written without the e when adding ing, an ending beginning with a vowel.
n<u>ight</u>	
pass	**Rule 17**
<u>sh</u>ut	

<u>ea</u>s y **<u>ea</u>se**₅	Write ease without the e when adding y, an ending beginning with a vowel. Add the base word when Rules 14, 15 and 16 apply. (Page 6 of the Notebook)

From now on add appropriate endings to base words in this list. This can soon be done independently in a separate period as a class assignment. A pupil should list no word he cannot use in a sentence.

birds[2]

bone

cloud

gar den

goose[5]

knife

mouth

oak

peach

pole

queen

rope

sea son[2]

space

stands[2]

wag on

wheat

win dow[2]

431 words are now in the notebooks. Only eleven of these words (of, one, said, eye, two, would, any, many, could, should and hour) cannot be made to agree in all their speech sounds with the phonograms in them.

Section L

catch
catch er
kitch en
bŭtch er

Pronounce the t in writing. tch is a phonogram but it is unnecessarily confusing for children. The tongue being at the same place for saying "t" "ch" forces the saying of only "ch" in catch, etch, witch, botch, clutch. Saying the "t" and "ch" for spelling in such words keeps children from putting "t" in words like much and which. The letters tch cannot be separated, however, and they always follow a single vowel which does not say ā, ē, ī, ō, ū (butch er, kitch en).

black

Rule 25

warm

un less

Rule 17

cloth ing

(Page 6 of the Notebook) Write clothe without the e to add ing, an ending beginning with a vowel.

clothe

be gan

be gin

be gun

a ble

gone₌₅

go

done₌₅

do³   (Say ŏ. "dun" is a color.)

suit²   (ui says "ū.")

track

wåtch³   (Pronounce t, in writing.)

dash

fell   **Rule 17**

fight

bu¹ y   (Sound "ŭ" in writing. Discuss meaning.)

by

stop

wålk³   (Sound as written for spelling. We say "wåk³,"
              "tåk³," "båk³.")

tålk³

bålk³

grant

s̲oap   This oa may be taught as the "ō" in the word
              boat.

ne̲w̲s̲

ne̲w

sma̲ll   **Rule 17** Also dictate smaller, smallest. The ll's
               remain in the first syllable.

wa̲r

sum me̲r

a̲ bov̲e̲   ex press   s cannot follow x.

tu̲rn   (Page 2 of the Notebook)

les son

ha̲lf   (Sound l, for spelling. We say "haf.")

fa̲ the̲r

a̲n y thi̲ng   (Say ă in writing.)

ta̲ bl̲e

hig̲h

ta̲lks   (Sound l in writing.)

June

Rule 26

right

write

wrote

date

road

rode

ride

March

Rule 26

march

next

in deed

four

her self

pow er

wish

be cause

cause

w**o**rld

c**ou**n try

[
m**ee**t

m**ea**t
]

an o**th** **er**

trip

list

p**e** **o** pl**e**   (Say three syllables for writing. We say "p**e** pl**e**." Among 1700 common words leopard is the only other word in which eo is a phonogram.)

ev **er**

held

chur**ch**   (Page 2 of the Notebook)

[
on**ce**   (Base word is one. Neither one nor once is pho- netic. We say "won**ce**" and "won.")

one
]

own

b**e** **fore**

[
kn**o**w

n**o**
]

were

where

(These four words have the same last three letters but they are not all said alike. Each is phonetic and has a final silent e.)

there

here

dead

leave

ear ly   (Page 2 in the Notebook)

close

close

flow er

flour   (The last sound is "r," not er. The word has only one syllable.)

noth ing

ground

lead   (the way)

led   (the way)

lead   (pen cil)

su<u>ch</u>

m<u>a</u>n y   (Say "ă," when writing. We say "men y.")

m<u>or</u>n <u>ing</u>

h<u>ow</u> ev <u>er</u>

mind   Rule 19

<u>sh</u>all   Rule 17

a lone

<u>or</u> der

<u>th</u>i<u>r</u>d   (Page 2 of the Notebook)

p<u>u</u><u>sh</u>

p<u>oi</u>nt

wi<u>th</u> in

bod y   (y says "ĭ.")

be long<u>s</u>

<u>chee</u>s<u>e</u>

<u>fea</u><u>th</u> <u>er</u>   (ea saying "ĕă" never ends a syllable.)

fence

hon <u>ey</u>

let ter$\overset{2}{\text{s}}$

$\overset{1}{\text{o}}$r an<u>ge</u>$_{\underset{=}{3}}$ (ŏ shows the phonogram is not <u>or</u>.)

po<u>ck</u> et

<u>ear</u>n   (Page 2 of the Notebook)

$\left[\begin{array}{l}\underline{\text{sh}}\overset{3}{\text{o}}\text{e}\overset{2}{\text{s}} \\ \\ \underline{\text{sh}}\overset{3}{\text{o}}\text{e}_{\underset{=}{5}}\end{array}\right.$

st<u>air</u>$\overset{2}{\text{s}}$

st<u>rea</u>m

t<u>i</u> ny

w<u>or</u>d$\overset{2}{\text{s}}$ (Page 2 of the Notebook)

First graders reach here by the middle of February if only thirty words a week were taught. Five hundred forty-four words are in their notebooks.

In the spelling lesson always ask the pupils to say polysyllable words in syllables. When the word is written, ask them to read it in syllables and then read it again as the word is said in proper English rhythm.

By now Rules 4, 5, 6, 7, 8, 17, 18, 19, 25 should be understood. They will no longer be noted.

The first grade now reviews as well as continues to learn the words in the list of Section O. Each day dictate five review words beginning with Sections A to H and ten review words beginning with Section I. These words should be written as a test on separate sheets (not in the notebook). Put in the notebooks thirty new words each week beginning with Section M. This permits reaching Section O by the middle of April. Then only those who need review can be helped and the others have more time to write compositions and read independently.

Section M

trust

ex trå³

dress

be̲ side̲

te̲a̲ch̲

hap pen

be̲ gun

col lect   (We often have the two sounds "c" and "t" at the end of a word: direct, elect, protect. Sound each carefully.)

fi̲le̲

pro̲ vi̲de̲

si̲ght

sto̲o̲d²

fix

fix**ed**

Rule 14 does not apply to words ending in x because x has *two* sounds, "ks" (ox, ox en).

born

goes

go

Have children say and write: Add **es** (say the names of e and s) to go, do and Tu to write goes, does and Tuesday.

does

do

Tues day

Tuesday is Tyr's day. Tyr was the Viking god of war. Four names of our days of the week are named for Viking gods. Wednesday is Woden's day. The Germans' name for Odin, the main god, was Woden. Thursday is Thor's day. He was the god of thunder. Friday is Frigga's day. She was the wife of Odin.

hold

drill

ar my

pret ty

(Say ĕ for writing only. We say "prit y.") **Rule 29**

stole

in come

(That which comes in.)

bought

paid pay   (The base words are pay, lay and say. We change the form of these words and do not add ed to the base words.)

laid lay

said say   (We write "said" but we say "sed." Both must be learned.)

en ter

rail road   (The rails are on the road.)

un a ble₄

tick et

ac count   We cannot say ā here. When the sound is definitely ă the vowel is followed by a consonant. (ăr rive, ăf fect, ăp pear) **Rule 29**

driv en

re al

re cov er

moun tain   (Sound it as it is written for spelling. Say the *ai* lightly in speaking.)

steam er

speak

past

m**igh**t

con tr**a**ct

d**ea**l

⌈ **ăl** most   **Rule 21**

⌊ **ăll**

br**oŭgh**t

less

e vent

⌈ off

⌊ o**f**

⌈ tr**ue**   Say ū for spelling.

⌊ tr**uth**   **Rule 19** The e is not needed here.

t**ŏŏ**k

a g**ai**n   (Sound it as it is written for spelling. We say "ā gĕn." The British say it as it is written.)

in f**o**rm

bo**th**   **Rule 19**

h**ear**t   (Not phonetic. We say "hart" but write heart. The doctor listens to your heart with his ear.)

mon<u>th</u>

[<u>ch</u>il dren

[<u>ch</u>ild   **Rule 19**

[bu̇¹ ild   (We say "bild" and "bilt.")

[bu̇¹ ilt

un d<u>er</u> stand

fol l<u>ow</u>²

<u>ch</u>arg<u>e</u>₃

[say<u>s</u>²   (Sound it as it is written for spelling. We say
                    "se<u>s</u>.²")

[s<u>ay</u>

mem b<u>er</u>

c<u>a</u>s<u>e</u>

w<u>hi</u>l<u>e</u>   (Not "wile ")

ål³ s<u>o</u>   **Rule 21**

r<u>e</u> t<u>ur</u>n   (Page 2 in Notebook)

of¹ fic<u>e</u>₃

gr<u>e</u>³at

Miss

miss

wh$\overset{3}{\underline{\underline{o}}}$ (Sound it as written for spelling. We say "h$\overset{3}{o}$.")

d$\overset{2}{\underline{ie}}\overset{2}{d}$ (The e serves two functions: ie says "ī" and ed says "d.")

d$\overset{2}{\underline{ie}}$ (Page 3 in the Notebook)

change

chang ing   (Page 6 in the Notebook) Change is written without the e. ing begins with i which permits the g to say "j," but the g is kept with the first syllable to preserve the meaning.

wire

fe$\overset{2}{\underline{w}}$ (ew says "ū.")

plea$\overset{2}{\underline{\underline{se}}}_{\underline{\underline{5}}}$

pic ture   Contrast pronunciation and meaning with pitcher.

pit$\underline{ch}$ **er**   A pitcher pitches a ball and a pitcher of milk pitches the liquid.

pit$\underline{ch}$

mon e$\overset{3}{\underline{y}}$ (ey says "ĭ.") The ey is changed to i and es is

mon ie$\overset{3}{\underline{}}\overset{2}{s}$ added for the plural. This is the only word where this is true: journeys, monkeys.

rĕad y

o mit

an y way   (Sound this compound word as it is written for spelling.)

a rith me tic

brĕak fast   (brĕak your fast)

freeze₅

broad   (Say "ō" for writing. In speech we say "ŏ," an uncommon sound for oa.)

chance₃

climb   **Rule 19**

cof fee

col or

con tains

dai ly   (Rule 24 does not hold here.)

day

ea gle₄

ex cuse

ex cuse

fan cy

[fas <u>ten</u>

fast]

fl<u>our</u>

fŏr est

gen tle₌₄

hole<u>s</u>²

ho<u>o</u> tel

<u>i</u> <u>ron</u>   (We say "<u>i</u> <u>ern</u>.")

[liv <u>ing</u>   (Page 6 in the Notebook)

live₌₂]

mon ke<u>y</u>³   (e<u>y</u>³ says ĭ.)

noi<u>se</u>²₌₅

<u>o</u> <u>ce</u>an   (Page 4 in the Notebook) <u>ce</u> is not often used
to say "sh."

pen cil

[<u>sew</u>   (n<u>ee</u> dl<u>e</u>²₌₄) (We write s<u>ew</u> but say "s<u>o</u>," an
uncommon sound for ew.)

sow²   (s<u>ee</u>d<u>s</u>²)

so<u>o</u>]

thre$\overset{2}{\text{a}}$d

thun d<u>er</u>

| tr<u>i</u>₂$\overset{2}{\text{e}}$d | **Rule 24** (e has two functions. The letters ie say ī and the ending says $\overset{2}{\text{e}}$d.) |
| try | |

Section N

ex cept

(c followed by e, i, or y may follow x. See Rule 20.)

| <u>au</u>nt | (Sound as written for spelling. Most people say "$\overset{3}{\text{a}}$nt." |
| ant | |

cap t<u>ure</u>

| <u>wrote</u> |
| <u>write</u> |

el<u>se</u>₅

bri<u>dg</u>e   Rule 23

of f<u>er</u>

suf f<u>er</u>

cen t<u>er</u>

front

r<u>ule</u>   (Say ū for spelling.)

c<u>a</u>[1]r ry   (<u>a</u>[1] is not part of <u>ar</u>.)

<u>ch</u>ain

d<u>ea</u>[2]th

l<u>ear</u>n   (Page 2 in the Notebook.)

won d<u>er</u>

t<u>i</u>r<u>e</u>

p<u>ai</u>r   (two)

p<u>ea</u>[3]r   (eat)

p<u>a</u>r<u>e</u>   (cut)

<u>ch</u>e<u>ck</u>

pr<u>o</u>[3]v<u>e</u>

h<u>ea</u>rd   (Page 2 in the Notebook.)

h<u>ea</u>r

in spect

it self

<u>a</u>[3]l way<u>s</u>[2]   Rule 21

som<u>e</u> <u>th</u>ing

ex pect   **Rule 20**

n<u>ee</u>d

th<u>us</u>[2]

wo man   (Sound as written for spelling. Came from wife
                          man.)

wo men   (We say "woom an" and "wim en." Both writ-
                          ing and pronunciation must be taught.)

y<u>oung</u>[4]

f<u>air</u>

f<u>are</u>

dol l<u>ar</u>

<u>eve</u> ning

<u>eve</u>

plan

br<u>oke</u>

f<u>ee</u>l

<u>sure</u>   (s says "sh," an uncommon sound. Say "s" for
                          writing.)

s<u>ug</u> <u>ar</u>[3]

least

sòr ry

press

God   Rule 26

god

t__each__ __er__

N__o__ vem b__er__   Rule 26   (This is the ninth month of the old Roman year. Novem means nine.)

sub ject

__A__ pril   Rule 26

his t__o__ ry

c__au__se   ₅

stud y

him self

mat t__er__

u__se__

th__ou__ght

p__er__ son

nor   (Explain the use of nor and or.)

or

Jan u ar y   **Rule 26** (Named for Roman god, Janus.)

mean

vote

court

cop y

act

been   (Sound as it is written for spelling. We say
                       "bin." The British say "been." Base word is
                       be.)

be

yes ter day

a mong

ques tion   (Sound as it is written for spelling. We say "ch"
                       here for ti.)

quest

doc tor

size   Few words use z except at the beginning of a
                       base word. Size, dozen, organize, citizen are
                       about the only ones in the first 1000 words.

De cem ber   **Rule 26** (This was the tenth month of the Roman calendar. Decem means ten.)

doz en

there

tax

num ber

Oc to ber   **Rule 26** (The eighth month of the Roman calendar. Octo means eight.)

rea son

fifth

bak ing   (Page 6 in the Notebook)

bake

cheap

cheer ful   **Rule 22**

chick en

driv ing   (Page 6 in the Notebook)

drive

ech o

ech oes   Add es (say the names of e and s) to echo. oe then says ō.

fair y

leath er   (ea saying ĕ never ends a syllable.)

lin en

mix ture

oys ter

peace₃

rough

smoke

steal

strange   The first function of the e is to let the a say ā. n and g have separate sounds.

vil lage

voice₃

voic es   (Page 6 in the Notebook) Voice is written without the e when adding "es," an ending beginning with a vowel. The c can still say "s." Show this by writing voi ces. For meaning we keep the c with the base word.

Grade 1 reaches here at mid-April (twenty-six weeks) by studying thirty words a week. Median spelling scores should be 3.4 or higher with none below 1.8. Much more reading by children from fine library books should be enjoyed before June, as well as reading aloud to the class by each pupil from sets of science books, stories based on history, myths, fairy tales and excellent poetry. Make time daily for the writing of original compositions of three or four sentences also.

Grade 2 studies the spelling words to Section R, page 214. After Christmas they are taught connected writing (pages 83–88) and thereafter use it exclusively in written work.

Grade 3 studies the words to Section V, but many third-graders can finish the list through Section Z.

Grade 4 and all older students need to finish the word list if their language skill is to be adequate for their required studies.

Section O

eight

ate

a fraid

un cle

rath er

com fort

e lect

a board   (This is the "ō" we use in boat. The use of the word boat should come to distinguish this spelling of "ō" from the several others.

jail

shed

re tire

re fuse

dis trict

re strain

roy al

For Grades 1 and 2 put on a corner of the chalkboard the phonograms ti, si and ci (pages 104, 105). Add the words containing these spellings as they are met, beginning with objection. See the notes to teachers.

ob jec tion   (Page 4 of the Notebook)

ob ject

pleas ure   (Comes from please.)

meas ure

treas ure

na vy

fourth

four

pop u la tion   (Page 4 of the Notebook)

prop er

judge

Rule 23

weath er

wheth er

The first sounds of these two words are different.

worth

(Page 2 of the Notebook)

con tain

fig ure

sud den

for ty

We say <u>or</u> in forty. The spelling shows this. In the other three words we say "ō."

four

fourth

four teen

in stead

throw

threw

per son al

ev er y thing

rate

(Page 3 of the Notebook) For Grade 2 put on paper the four headings from pages 100 and 101. Read the notes on page 102. Put chief in the first column and add in the proper columns words containing ie and ei as they are met.

Grade 3 and older students should have all the words on pages 100 and 101 dictated to them. See the notes on page 102.

All seven pages are now complete in the front of their notebooks. These are all shown in Chapter IV and should be referred to whenever they can answer any problem in speech, writing, or reading. Each of these pages should become so familiar to each student that the mention for example, of ie and ei makes it unnecessary for him to turn to Page 3. When he is writing or reading each pupil's notebook should be a readily available source of information until all the facts in it are automatically used by him.

chief   (Page 3 of the Notebook)

per fect

sec ond

slide

far ²ther

du ty

in tend

com pan y

quite

quit

qui et

none⁼₅

knew

know

re main

di rect   (i says ĭ.)

di rec tion   (Page 4 in the Notebook)

ap pear

lib er ty

e nough

fact

board   (We use the ō of boat.)

Sep tem ber

sta tion   (Page 4 of the Notebook)

at tend

be tween

pub lic

mu sic

pic nic   When adding ing we write ck to keep the "k" sound (picnick ing).

friend

friends²

(Page 3 of the Notebook) The double line indicates only that ĕ is an uncommon sound for ie.

dur² ing

en dure

through²

po lice

(Say the word as it is written for spelling. We say "po lece," using the French i saying "ē.")

un til

Rule 22

mad am

tru ly

true₂

(Learn to write true without the e when writing truly. The e is used at the end of true because we do not end words with a single u. In truly it is no longer needed, even though the ending does not begin with a vowel.)

whole

(Sound as it is written for spelling.)

hole

ad dress

re quest

raise²₅

Au gust

stru<u>ck</u>

get <u>t</u><u>ing</u>   (Page 5 in the Notebook)

get

don't = dŏ³ not   **Rule 19** The apostrophe shows where the letter
                              o has been left out. Don't is a contrac-
                              tion of two one-syllable words into a
                              one-syllable word.)

Thur<u>s</u>² <u>day</u>   (Page 2 in the Notebook) (Thursday is Thor's
                              day.)

Sat <u>ur</u> <u>day</u>   (Saturday is Saturn's day.)

cá¹ nōe³₌₅

cap <u>tain</u>

cel <u>lar</u>

cl<u>o</u>²<u>the</u>²<u>s</u>

cl<u>o</u>²<u>the</u>²

cov <u>ere</u>²<u>d</u>

cr<u>ea</u> <u>ture</u>

c<u>ur</u> <u>tain</u>   (Page 2 in the Notebook)

d<u>e</u> cl<u>are</u>²<u>d</u>   (Page 6 in the Notebook)

d<u>e</u> cl<u>are</u>

dis tance‗₃

dis tant

ex pl<u>ai</u>n — Rule 20

f<u>ie</u>ld<u>s</u>² — (Page 3 in the Notebook)

fl<u>oat</u> <u>ed</u> — Rule 28

hol i d<u>ay</u>

h<u>o</u> ly

lem on

l<u>y</u> <u>ing</u>

l<u>ie</u>² — (Page 3 in the Notebook)

m<u>ou</u>n t<u>ai</u>n<u>s</u>²

n<u>ai</u>l<u>s</u>²

n<u>ee</u> dl<u>e</u>‗₄

n<u>o</u> bod y

<u>oar</u>

pal ace‗₃

pen ny

reg <u>u</u> l<u>ar</u>

re peats

re prove

sail or

sen tence

shin ing   (Page 6 in the Notebook)

shine

sur face   (Page 2 in the Notebook)

sweep ing

sweeps

thief   (Page 3 in the Notebook)

waist

waste   Two separate consonant sounds come between
the a and the e which lets it say "$\bar{a}$."

wait ing

wea ry

writ ing   (Page 6 in the Notebook)

writ er   (Page 6 in the Notebook)

write

Section P

spend

en joy

aw fŭl

Rule 22 Since the e of awe has no function, awful is written without the e, even though the ending ful does not begin with a vowel.

awe

u šu al

com plaint

au to

va ca tion

bea u ti fŭl

(Sound as it is written for spelling. We say "bu ti fŭl." eau is a French phonogram.)

bea u ty

flight

trav el

rap id

re pair

trou̲⁴ ble̲=₄

trou̲⁴ bli̲ng̲   (This word has only two syllables.)

en tra̲nce̲-=₃

im po̲r tance̲-=₃

im po̲r tant

ca̅r¹ ri̲e̲ed³²   **Rule 24** (The ie says "ī" and ed says "d." The e
                        has two functions.)

ca̅r¹ ry   (y says "ī.")

lo̲ss̲

fo̲r tu̲ne̲

em pi̲re̲

ma̲y̲ o̲r

wa̲it

beg

de̲ gre̲e̲

pri̲s̲² on

en gi̲ne̲=₅

vi̲s̲² it

guest   (Teach gu as a phonogram saying "g." If the g were next to the e it could say "j.")

guess

de part ment

ob tain

fam i ly

an i mal

fa vor

Mrs.   (The period means that some letters of the word are not written. Mrs. is an abbreviation for which we say "Mis is" in speaking.)

Mr. = Mis ter   (Here the first and last letters form the abbreviation.)

Miss   (Needs no period since the whole word is written.)

hus band   (A husband gives his wife a band ring.)

a mount

hu man

vi ew   (The dictionary gives "vū." Sound the ĭ for spelling.)

e lec tion   (The t of elect went over to form ti.)

e lect

clerk

though

o'clock   (Means "of the clock." f and the are left out in this contraction of three words to a word of two syllables.)

sup port

does   (Add es to do and go to write does and goes.)

goes

re gard

es cape

since

which   (Not witch)

length   Sound ng correctly.

long

strength

strong

de stroy

news pa per

daugh ter

(Few words use augh. Teach this phonogram saying "au." Its spelling is similar to the more common igh, eigh and ough.)

naugh ty

caught

taught

an swer

(Sound the w when writing until the spelling is learned.)

re ply

o blige

(We would not use dge here since we say "ī.")

sail

sale

cit ies

Rule 24 Change the y of city to i and add es. (Say the names of e and s.) The ie says "ĭ," as does the y of city.

cit y

known

know

sev er al

de sire

near ly

ba sin

butch er

but ton

cab bage

care ful

Rule 22

laugh

(Say "auf" for writing. Most Americans say "lăf.")

laugh ter

cough

cous in

dol lars

freeze

grief

(Page 3 in the Notebook)

guil ty

hop ping

(Page 5 in the Notebook)

hop

hun gry

kit<u>ch</u> en

lan <u>guage</u>　　　　(gu says "gw.") The u says "w" as it does in qu ("kw").

⎡ lin <u>ing</u>　　　　(Page 6 in the Notebook)

⎣ l<u>i</u><u>n</u><u>e</u>

ne<u>ph</u> <u>e</u>w²

n<u>ine</u> t<u>ee</u>n

⎡ n<u>o</u> tic<u>e</u>d³　　　　(Page 6 in the Notebook)

⎣ n<u>o</u> tic<u>e</u>₃

p<u>ar</u> l<u>or</u>

pas sen g<u>er</u>s²

<u>qu</u>eer

r<u>e</u> m<u>ai</u>n<u>e</u>d²

r<u>e</u> tr<u>ea</u>t <u>ing</u>

st<u>y</u><u>l</u>e

sub tract

t<u>ai</u> l<u>or</u>

<u>th</u>um<u>b</u>

tills²

tri al

twelve₂

voy age

whis per

wrong

Section Q

some times²

de clare

en gage

fi nal

ter ri ble₄

sur prise²   (Page 2 in the Notebook)

pe ri od

ad di tion

em ploy

prop er ty

se lect

con nec tion

con nect

firm   (Page 2 in the Notebook)

re gion   (gi says "j." Without the i the last syllable
                              would say "gon.")

re li gion

con vict

pri vate

com mand

de bate

crowd

fac to ry

pub lish   Rule 10

rep re sent

term   (Page 2 in the Notebook)

sec tion

rel a tive

re late

⎡ **prog ress**   (Noun)

⎣ **pr͟o gress**   (Verb)

   en t͟i͟r͟e

⎡ **pre͟s̲ i dent**

⎣ **pr͟e s̲͟i͟d͟e**

   me͟a̲s̲ u͟r͟e

⎡ **f͟a mo͟u̲s**   (ous means full of; famous means full of fame.)

⎣ **f͟a͟m͟e**

   s͟e͟r͟v͟e   (Page 2 in the Notebook)

   es t͟a͟t͟e

   r͟e mem b͟e͟r

   e͟i t̲her   (Page 3 in the Notebook)

   ef f͟o͟rt

⎡ **im p͟o͟r tant**

⎣ **im p͟o͟r tanc͟e**

⎡ **du͟e͟**

⎣ **de̲w͟**

in cl**ude**

run **ning** (Page 5 in the Notebook) The second n in running is not the same as the two l's in allow. The second n in running is a reasoned one which the child must remember to write.

run

al **low** **Rule 29**

po si tion

field (Page 3 in the Notebook)

ledge **Rule 23**

cl**ai**m

pri ma ry

re sult

Sat **ur** d**ay** (Page 2 in the Notebook)

ap p**oi**nt **Rule 29**

in f**or** ma **tion**

whom (Sound as written for spelling. We say "hŏm.")

who

ar rest **Rule 29**

them selves   (Learn: Change "f" of self to "v" and add es. Say
                      the names of e and s.)

self

calves   (Sound the l for spelling.)

calf

halves   (Sound the l for spelling.)

half

spe cial   e says "ĕ" here. (Page 4 in the Notebook) Rule 11

es pe cial ly

pres ent   (Noun)

pre sent   (Verb)

ac tion

act

jus tice

just

gen tle man

gen tle

en close

a w<u>ai</u>t

sup p<u>o</u><u>s</u>e²

won d<u>er</u> fu̇l³   Rule 22

[f<u>or</u> w<u>ar</u>d

  ba<u>ck</u> w<u>ar</u>d

  t<u>o</u> w<u>ar</u>d   (Sound as written for spelling. We say "t<u>o</u> <u>ar</u>d.")

<u>al</u>³ <u>th</u>ough²   Rule 21

prompt   (Sound p and t carefully.)

at tempt   Rule 29

[<u>wh</u>o<u>s</u>e³²₌₅   (Sound as written and then say "ho̊s.³²")

  <u>wh</u>o̊³

[st<u>ate</u> ment

  st<u>ate</u>

p<u>er</u> haps

[<u>th</u>e<u>i</u>r²²   (Page 3 in the Notebook)

  <u>th</u>ey²

im pri<u>s</u>² on

writ ten | (Page 5 in the Notebook) Think of the archaic form writ as the base word.

writ

ar range | (The first a says "ă." The second a has two separate consonants between it and the silent e.)

an kle

ap pears | Rule 29

beg gar | (Page 5 in the Notebook) Rule 29.

beg

brace let

brace

breathe

breath

calm

cir cus | (Page 2 in the Notebook.)

con sent ed

con tin ued | (Page 6 in the Notebook)

con tin ue

dan ger ous

de**bt**

[**dri̱e̱d**   **Rule 24** (Page 3 in the Notebook)

dry̱

ex **e̱r** **ci̱s̱e**

gram **ma̱r**

Iṉ di an   **Rule 26**

[**jou̱r** ne̱y   Teach **ou̱r** as a phonogram saying "ur." The British use this spelling more than do Americans.

co̱u̱r **a̱g̱e**

jou̱r nal

[**la̱i̱d**

la̱y

pra̱i̱s̱e

prop **e̱r** ly

se̱a̱ṟcẖe̱d   (Page 2 in the Notebook)

smo̱o̱tẖ

thi̱r **te̱e̱n**   (Page 2 in the Notebook)

to̱u̱ch

t<u>ow</u> el

um brel l<u>a</u>³   (a says "a̧³" at the end of a word, never "ā," ex-
                                  cept in the article a.)

v<u>ea</u>l

w<u>ĕ</u>²<u>a</u>p on

Grade 2 reaches here before June.

Section R

fore n<u>oo</u>n   (before noon)

b<u>e</u> f<u>ore</u>

l<u>o</u>³²<u>se</u>₅   (Verb)

l<u>oo</u>se₅   t<u>oo</u>th   (Teach "loose tooth." Both words use oo to say
                                  "o̅o̅.")

loss

com bi n<u>a</u> <u>t</u>ion

com b<u>ine</u>

av e̊¹ n<u>ue</u>₂

neigh b<u>or</u>

w<u>eigh</u>

w<u>ĕ</u>³<u>a</u>r

en ter tain

sal a ry

vis i tor

vis it

pub li ca tion

ma chine   (Sound as written for spelling. We say "mă shēn," using the French "ē" for i.)

en gine

suc cess

drown

a dopt

se cure

hon or   (Sound the h for spelling.)

prom ise

wreck

pre pare

ves sel

bus y   (Sound as written for spelling and then read "bis y."

pre fer

pref er ence₃   (This does not follow Rule 15. The accent changes.)

il lus trate

il lus tra tion

dif fer ent

dif fer

ob ject

pro vi sion   (Page 4 in the Notebook)

ac cord ing

al read y   Rule 21

at ten tion

ed u ca tion

di rec tor

di rect

pur pose₅   (Page 2 in the Notebook)

com mon

di a mond

to geth er

con ven <u>tion</u>

in cr<u>ea</u>s<u>e</u>₌₅

man n<u>er</u>

<u>fea</u> <u>ture</u>

<u>ar</u> ti cl<u>e</u>₌₄

s<u>er</u>v ic<u>e</u>₌₃   (Page 6 in the Notebook)

s<u>erve</u>₌₂

in j<u>ure</u>

in j<u>u</u> ry

ef fect   Rule 29

dis trib <u>ute</u>

gen <u>er</u> al

to m³or r²<u>ow</u> ₁

con sid <u>er</u>

<u>a</u> g<u>ai</u>nst   (Sound as written for spelling. Then read "ā-genst.")

<u>a</u> g<u>ai</u>n   (Sound as written for spelling. Then read "ā-gen.")

g<u>ai</u>n

com pl<u>ete</u>

<u>sear</u>ch   (Page 2 in the Notebook)

pop <u>u</u> l<u>ar</u>

<u>Chr</u>ist mas   **Rule 22**   (The Mass of Christ. Sound t for spelling.)

<u>Chr</u>ist   **Rules 19 and 26**

in t<u>er</u> est

ad v<u>ice</u>

ad vi<u>se</u>

<u>A</u> mer i can   (e says "ĕ.")

<u>A</u> mer i c<u>a</u>

b<u>ar</u> g<u>ai</u>n

<u>choose</u>

c<u>o</u> c<u>oa</u>

col l<u>ar</u>   **Rule 19**

de<u>b</u>ts

di<u>s</u> as t<u>er</u>

en <u>e</u> my

fierce₃   (Page 3 in the Notebook)

jan i tor

law yer

⎡ pa tient   (Page 4 in the Notebook)

⎣ pa tience₃

⎡ pi an´ o

  pi an´ os   The accent is on the second syllable in each of
                     these words. Musical terms ending in o add s to
                     form plurals: solos, altos.

⎣ pi an´ ist

⎡ pick les

⎣ pick le₄

pris on er

re lease₅

re sign   **Rule 19**

re veal

sleeve₂

sol dier   (di = "j.")

stop ping   (Page 5 in the Notebook)

stop

sword

to bac co

trea son

to ma to

to ma toes   Add es (say the names of e and s) to form the
                    plural.

Section S

of ten   (Sound t for spelling. Then say "of en.")

stopped   (Page 5 in the Notebook)

stop

mo tion

the a ter   (Be sure to accent the first syllable in speech:
                    the' a ter.)

im prove ment

im prove

cen tu ry

cent

to tal

men tion

ar rive   Rule 29

sup ply

as sist   Rule 29

dif fer ence₃

ex am i na tion   (Sound as written for spelling. We say "eg zam i na tion.")

ex am ine₅

par tic u lar

af fair   Rule 29

course₅

coarse₅   (Not fine)

nei ther   (Page 3 in the Notebook)

lo cal

mar ri age   (Sound in three syllables for spelling. Then say "măr age.")

mar ry   Rule 29

căr ri age   (Sound as written for spelling. Then say "căr
                              age.)

căr ry

fur ther   (Page 2 in the Notebook)

se ri ous

doubt   (Sound b for spelling)

con di tion

gov ern ment   ("ern," not "er.")

gov ern

o pin ion   In these eight words the i of the last syllable is a
                              consonant, saying the consonant sound "y." i is
                              also part of the consonant phonograms ti, si, ci
                              and gi (region).

on ion

un ion

fa mil iar

be hav ior   (Page 6 in the Notebook)

com pan ion

mil lion

pe cul iar

be lieve$_2$ (Page 3 in the Notebook)

sys tem

pos si ble$_4$

pos si bly

piece$_3$ (Page 3 in the Notebook)

peace$_3$

cer tain   (Page 2 in the Notebook)

wit ness

in ves ti gate

there fore$_5$

be fore

too   Means: also, or more than enough.

two^3

to^3

an xious^4 (x = "ks", xi = "ksi" = "ksh".) (Page 4 in the Notebook.) The dictionary division is anx ious. n before the sounds "k" and "g" = "ng."

can vas

ceil ing   (Page 3 in the Notebook)

cel <u>er</u> y

sal <u>a</u> ry

c<u>er</u> t<u>ai</u>n ly   (Page 2 in the Notebook)

col l<u>eg<u>e</u></u>=3

com rad<u>e</u>=5

con c<u>er</u>t

d<u>e</u> cid <u>ed</u>   (Page 6 in the Notebook)

d<u>e</u> c<u>id</u>e

d<u>e</u> s<u>ig</u>n²   Rule 19

dic <u>t</u>ion àr¹ y

el <u>e</u> <u>ph</u>ant

<u>fer</u> til<u>e</u>=5

f<u>r</u>i<u>ght</u> en<u>ed</u>²

gal lo<u>w</u>s² ²

g<u>ro</u> c<u>er</u> y

han<u>d</u> k<u>er</u> <u>ch</u>i<u>ef</u>³   (Page 3 in the Notebook)

lis t<u>en<u>ed</u></u>²

m<u>or</u> sel

ni<u>ck</u> el

niece=3   (Page 3 in the Notebook)

pis tols²

[pur chased³   (Pages 2 and 6 in the Notebook)

pur chase

quar rel

re cess

sau cer

sleigh

so ci e ty¹

source² -=3

speech

st ea k³

tel e phone

trol ley³

whis tle ==4

Section T

[cir cu lar   (Page 2 in the Notebook)

cir cle=4

ar gu ment

(Learn to write argue without the e. We need the e in argue, only because a u should not end a word.)

ar gue₂

vol ume

or gan ize

sum mon

of fi cial

(Page 4 in the Notebook) **Rule 29**

of fi cer

(Page 6 in the Notebook)

of fice₃

vic tim

es ti mate

ac ci dent

in vi ta tion

in vite

ac cept

im pos si ble₄

con cern

au to mo bile₅

as so ci ate   (Page 4 of the Notebook) ci, a syllable alone, says "shĭ." The i serves two functions since there is no other vowel sound like the "ă" in cial of official. **Rule 29**

as so ci a tion   (c and i are separate phonograms saying "cĭ.")

văr i ŏus

văr y

vĕr y

de cide

de ci sion   (Page 4 of Notebook)

en ti tle

po lit i cal

nā tion al

na tion

re cent

bŭs i ness   (Sound as written for spelling. We say "bĭs ness.")

bŭs y

re fer

min ute

mi nute

ou̲g̱h̲t

[ab sence

  ab sent

[con fe̲r ence   (Does not follow Rule 15. The accent shifts to
                          con′ and we do not double the r.)

  con fe̲r

Wed̲ nes̲ da̲y   (Sound as written for spelling. This is Woden's
                          day. We say "Wens̃ day.")

[re̱ al ly

  re̱ al

cel e̱ bra̲ tion̲

[folḵs   (Sound 1 when spelling.)

  folḵ   **Rule 19**

[ac̲h̲es

  ac̲h̲e

a̱ mus̱e ment

[ap pro̊v al   (Page 6 in the Notebook)

  ap pro̊ve

bå nan å

bis cuits   We write cu to say "k." This is like writing gu to say "g" in guess.

bruised   (Page 6 in the Notebook)

bruise

bur glar

change a ble   **Rule 3**   (Rule 16 cannot be applied here.)

chim ney

choir   We say "quire." That spelling means twenty-four sheets of paper. Choir and chorus are related in meaning and in some letters used in writing, but not in the sounds they say.

com mence

com pete

de ceive   (Page 3 in the Notebook)

dis cov er ies   (Page 3 in Notebook)

e lec tric i ty

er ror

err   **Rule 17**

ex cep tions

fa vor ite

gen u ine=5

hand fŭl   **Rule 22**

hymn

in ves ti ga tion

⎡ lil ĭĕs   (Page 3 in the Notebook)

⎣ lil y

li q̆uor   (Page 7 in the Notebook) qu says "k." Dictate the five phonograms to be put at the bottom of Page 7 in the students' notebooks. Use the notes to teachers on page 118. The words illustrating these phonograms may be dictated also. Page 7 will be referred to when one of these phonograms is used. The dictionary division is li q̆uor.

med al

med i cine=5

nine ty

re al ize

rĕign   (Page 3 in the Notebook)

se vere

⎡ slippĕd   (Page 5 in the Notebook)

⎣ slip

sneeze

sta tion ar y   (Won't move)

sta tion er y   (Note paper)

stom ach

straight   (Few words use this four-letter "ā." The common phonograms igh, eigh, ough are on the 70 phonogram cards. augh saying "au" and "auf" and now aigh saying "ā" have been added.)

suc ceed

tel e gram

whis tling   (Page 6 in the Notebook) There are but two vowels in this word. It has two syllables, not three.

whis tle

whole some

wreath

wres tle

Section U

meant

mean

ear li est   **Rule 24**

ear ly   (Page 2 in the Notebook)

wheth er

dis tin guish   (gu in guess said "g." Here the u says "w" as it
                              does in qu, "kw." We say "dis ting gwish.")

con sid er a tion

col o nies   **Rule 24** (Change y to i and add es.)

col o ny

co lo ni al   **Rule 24**

as sure   (s says "sh.") **Rule 29**

sure

re lief   (Page 3 in the Notebook)

oc cu py

prob a bly

prob a ble

for eign   (Page 3 in the Notebook) ei says "ī."

ex pense   **Rule 20**

re spon si ble   (Page 6 in the Notebook)

re sponse

be gin ning

(Page 5 in the Notebook) If the second half of Page 5 has not yet been put in the notebooks of third-graders and older students, dictate it now. See pages 107, 108 and 110.

be gin

ap pli ca tion

ap ply

dif fi cul ty

dif fi cult

scene

(These words use sc to say "s." s always says "s" at the beginning of a word. Since e or i follows the c it must say "s." This can be likened to ck. c and k alone say "k" and when used together they say "k.")

scen er y

(Page 6 in the Notebook)

sci ence

scis sors

Rule 29

de scend

as cend

(The s with the a indicates the a says ă. Rule 29 holds here because s and c have the same sound.)

de scent

as cent

⎡ fi̱ nal ly

⎣ fi̱ nal

⎡ de̱ vel op

⎢⎡ en vel op   (Verb)

⎣⎣ en vel o̲p̲e̲   (Noun)

⎡ ci̲r cum stan̲c̲e̲₃   (Page 2 in the Notebook)

⎢ ci̲r cum fe̲r enc̲e̲₃

⎣ ci̲r cle̲₄

⎡ i̲s̲ su̲e̲₂   s says "sh" (s̲u̲r̲e̲ and sů̲g a̲r) (Rule 29) The sound
⎢   of the second s̲ drop̲s̲ out in speech.

⎣ ti̲s su̲e̲₂

ma̍ te̱ ri al

sug gest

me̲r̲e̲

⎡ sen at̲e̲₅

⎢ sen a̲ to̲r

⎢

⎣ sen a̲ to̲ ri al

re̲ ce̲i̲v̲e̲₂   (Page 3 in the Notebook)

re spect fŭl ly   ly is an ending and both l's are sounded. Rule 29
does not apply.

re spect fŭl

re spect

a gree ment

a gree

un for tu nate

ma jŏr i ty

ma jor

e lab o rate

cit i zen

cit y

nec es sar y

ne ces si ty

di vide

a chieves   (Page 3 in the Notebook)

a chieve

ac quire

ạl mà nac

ản cient   (Page 4 in the Notebook)

a piece   (Page 3 in the Notebook)

ap proach es

at tor ney   (or says "ur.")

bou quet   (Page 7 in the Notebook) et says "ā" in this French word.

cal cu la tion

cer e mo ny

con cealed

de li cious   (Page 4 in the Notebook)

de scribed   (Page 6 in the Notebook)

de scribe

dis ap pear

dropped   (Page 5 in the Notebook)

drop

el e gant

em p<u>er</u> <u>or</u>

em p<u>er</u> <u>or</u>

ex c<u>el</u> lent   The accent is on ex in this word.

ex cel

gr<u>ate</u> fŭl

h<u>ei</u>r   (Page 3 in the Notebook)

h<u>oa</u>rse

<u>i</u> ci <u>cle</u>

ig n<u>o</u> ran<u>ce</u>

ig n<u>o</u> rant

ig n<u>ore</u>

in t<u>er</u> f<u>ere</u>

in t<u>er</u> fer en<u>ce</u>   (Page 6 in the Notebook)

mu si <u>c</u>ian   (Page 4 in the Notebook)

n<u>eu</u> tral   (Page 7 in the Notebook)

p<u>a</u> t<u>ien</u><u>ce</u>   (Page 4 in the Notebook)

pi <u>ge</u>ons   (ge says "j.")

r<u>e</u> h<u>ear</u>se   (Page 2 in the Notebook)

rev <u>er</u> ence₌₃

rev <u>er</u> ent

r<u>e</u> v<u>ere</u>

s<u>au</u> cy

si<u>ege</u>₌₃   (Page 3 in the Notebook)

veg <u>e</u> t<u>a</u> bl<u>e</u>₌₄

v<u>ea</u>l

<u>wretch</u>

Section V

prin ci pal   (main)

prin ci pl<u>e</u>₌₄   (theory)

tes ti m<u>o</u> ny

dis cus <u>sion</u>   (Page 4 in the Notebook.)

dis cu<u>ss</u>

ar r<u>ange</u> ment   **Rule 29**

ar r<u>ange</u>   (Here two separate consonants "n" and "j" come between a, which says "ā," and the final e.)

ref <u>er</u> en<u>ce</u>₃   (Rule 15 does not work here. The accent shifted to the first syllable and we do not double the r.)

r<u>e</u> f<u>er</u>

ev i den<u>ce</u>₃

ex p<u>e</u> ri en<u>ce</u>₃

ses <u>sion</u>   (Page 4 in the Notebook)

sec r<u>e</u> t<u>a</u>r y

c<u>a</u> r<u>eer</u>

<u>height</u>   (We write an ā sound but we say "ī.")

<u>weight</u>

ap p<u>a</u>r ent   Rule 29

<u>ar</u> til l<u>er</u> y   Rule 29

cam p<u>aig</u>n

c<u>e</u> r<u>e</u> al

col umn<u>s</u>

de s<u>ir</u> <u>a</u> bl<u>e</u>₄   (Page 6 in the Notebook)

d<u>e</u> s<u>ire</u>

ex tr<u>eme</u>   Rule 20

hom i ny

im ag ine₅   (Page 6 in the Notebook)

im age

in de pend ent

in di vid u al

in no cent

lei šure   (Page 3 in the Notebook)

li cense₅

mag nif i cent

mos qui to   (Page 7 in the Notebook) Spanish i says "ē."
For spelling say "ī."

mys te ri ous

oc ca sion   (Page 4 in the Notebook)

prai rie   (Page 3 in the Notebook)

re lieve₂   (Page 3 in the Notebook)

sac ri fice

sen si ble₄   (Page 6 in the Notebook)

sense₅

sol emn̲̲

ty̲ in̲g	
tie̲²	(Page 3 in the Notebook.)

va̍¹ lise̲̲ ₅   (French i saying ē: "va̍ lēs.")

vol un te̲er

wel fa̲re̲   **Rule 22**

ya̍³c̲h̲t

Section W

o̲r gan i za̲ ti̲on	
o̲r gan iz̲e̲	

e̲ me̲r gen cy

ap pre̲ ci̲ ate̲   (Page 4 in the Notebook) Since ci is a syllable alone it says "shĭ" instead of just "sh" as in ancie̲nt. (Rule 29)

sin cere̲ ly	(ly begins with a consonant. Sincere retains the final e.)
sin cere̲	

at̲h̲ let ic
at̲h̲ lete̲

flu̲ o̲ res cent

prac ti cal

pr<u>o</u> <u>c</u>eed

c<u>or</u> <u>d</u>ial ly   <u>di</u> = "j" as in sol <u>dier</u>

c<u>or</u> <u>d</u>ial

ch²¹ar ac <u>t</u>er

act

sep <u>a</u> r<u>ate</u>

Feb r<u>u</u> ăr y

l<u>i</u> brăr y

im m<u>e</u> di <u>ate</u>

con vĕn <u>i</u>ent   (The i says the consonant y sound as in opin<u>i</u>on shown before.)

r<u>e</u> <u>c</u>ei<u>p</u>t   (Page 3 in the Notebook) Sound the p for spelling. We do not say it in speech. Receipt was once recipe.

pr<u>e</u> lim i năr y

dis ap p<u>oi</u>nt

es pĕ <u>c</u>ial ly   (Page 4 in the Notebook)

spĕ <u>c</u>ial

an n<u>u</u> al

com mit tee

em ploy ee

(Except in a few words [recipē and apostrophē are two exceptions] we use ee, ea, or ey to say "ē" at the end of a word of more than one syllable. Single e's are silent at the end of other words. Very few one-syllable words end with a single e saying ē: me, we, he, she, be.)

cof fee

an tique

(Page 7 in the Notebook) French i = "ē."

bi cy cle

(bi means 2. tri means 3.)

tri an gle

cal en dar

con se quence

dis ease

(dis = no.)

fa tigue

French i says "ē." We have had three other French words where i = "ē": machine, valise and antique.

for eign ers

(Page 3 in the Notebook)

grease

(Noun and verb)

isth mus

non sense

(non = no)

re sourc es

(Page 6 in the Notebook)

re source

ve hi cle₄

vi cin i ty

ar chi² tec ture

ar ti fi cial   (Page 4 in the Notebook)

ben e fi cial   (Page 4 in the Notebook)

ben e fit

col o nel   For spelling say what is written. We say "ker nel." choir and colonel are two words in 1700 with truly bizarre spellings.

con fec tion¹ er y

con ta gious⁴

de vel op ment

de vel op

dis till er y

dis till

em ploy ees²

ex qui site²₅

in tel li gent

mis tle toe₄

op por tu ni ty   (Page 6 in the Notebook)

op por tune

per se vere

re proach[3]ed

rins[3]ed   (Page 6 in the Notebook)

rinse[=5]

tre[2]ach er y

Section X

de ci [2]sion   Rule 13

de cide

ac com mo date

ac cu ra cy   Rule 29

coun ter fe[3]it   (Page 3 in the Notebook)

des[2] sert[2]   Rule 29

des[2] ert   (A "des[2] ert" is a "de [2]sert ed" place and has but one s.)

di gest i ble[=4]

di gest   (Verb)

di gest   (Noun) A digest of a longer writing.

im mense

le o pard   (We say "lĕ p<u>ar</u>d.")

mar mă lade

mil lion aire   (i = "y.") **Rule 29**

mu ci lage

or ches tră

par li a ment   (We say "p<u>ar</u> li ment.")

per ceived   (Pages 3 and 6 in the Notebook)

per ceive

pos sess   **Rule 29**

prec i pice

pre cip i tous

rec om mend   (There is but one c. "<u>re</u> com mend" is the meaning.)

re sem blance   (Page 6 in the Notebook)

re sem ble

res tau rant

seized   (Pages 3 and 6 in the Notebook)

seize

su per in tend ent

sur geon   (Page 2 in the Notebook) ge says "j."

thor ough ly   (or says "ur" in this accented syllable.)

Section Y

judg ment   (dg here should not say "j." This is a rare excep-
                      tion to Rule 3.)

judge

al lege   Rule 29

al le giance

ac quaint ance

cem e ter y

e lim i nate

en deav or

en thu si asm

ex traor di nar y   There are but 5 syllables.

mil li ner y   Rule 29

mil li ner

mort gage

par al lel

phy s̆i cian   (Page 4 in the Notebook) Words containing y
                      where we expect i stem from the Greek.

por ce lain

rec i pe

⎡ syl la bles̆

⎣ syl la ble

tor toise   (We say "tor tus.")

a pol o gize

⎡ ap pro pri ate   (Verb) **Rule 29**

⎣ ap pro pri ate   (Adjective)

cau li flow er

chan de lier   (Page 3 in the Notebook)

dis ci pline

⎡ dis pen sa ry

⎣ dis pen sa tion

⎡ fa ti guing   (Page 6 in the Notebook) French i says "ē."

⎣ fa tigue

im me di ate ly

ker o sene

mé nag er ïe   (Page 3 in the Notebook)

mu nic i pal

mis chïe vous   (Page 3 in the Notebook) Sound "f" of chief changes to sound "v."

mis chïef   (Page 3 in the Notebook)

per sist ence₃

priv i lege₃

tran quil

tran quil li ty

suf fi cient ly   (Page 4 in the Notebook)

vague ly

vague

Section Z

com bus ti ble₄

guar an tee

in ces sant

oc cur rence₃   (Pages 2 and 5 in the Notebook)

pro fi cien cy   (Page 4 in the Notebook)

pro fi cient

vil l<u>ai</u>n

<u>a</u> byss   Rule 17

can t<u>a</u> l<u>o</u>²<u>u</u>pe₌₅

[em b<u>a</u>¹r rass ment

[em b<u>a</u>¹r rass   Rule 17

p<u>o</u>²<u>u</u>l tice₋₌₃

sov <u>er</u> <u>ei</u>³gn   (Page 3 in the Notebook)

[syn di c<u>ate</u>   (Verb)

[syn di c<u>ate</u>₌₅   (Noun)

ap pen di c<u>i</u> tis

č hauf fe ur   (We say "č h<u>o</u>³ f<u>ur</u>.")
<u>c</u>   <u>h</u> <u>e</u> <u>u</u>

hip p<u>o</u> pot <u>a</u> mus

[m<u>a</u>¹ n<u>eu</u> ver   (Page 7 in the Notebook)

[n<u>eu</u> tral

[<u>Eu</u> r<u>o</u>pe

[pn<u>eu</u> m<u>o</u> ni a³

[li <u>eu</u> ten ant   (We say "l<u>eu</u> ten ant.")

mis cel l<u>a</u> n<u>e</u> <u>ou</u>⁴s

pen i ten t<u>ia</u>³ ry   (Page 4 in the Notebook)

sou ve nir

hal le lu jahs   (j = "y")

flam ma ble

rhi noc er os   (Page 7 in the Notebook)

rhap so dy

rheu mat ic

con sci en tious   (Page 4 in the Notebook)

dis cern i ble

dis sen sion   (Page 4 in the Notebook)

jar di niere   (Page 3 in the Notebook)

chan de lier

fin an cier   An exception, a rare one, to Rule 9.

naph tha

ren dez vous   (We say "ran da vou.")

The constant growth of each student in learning to say and write from dictation the 1700 words with their endings and prefixes, listed in this chapter provide him with a basic mastery of English words. Every student needs to know all of them at least by sixth grade. Teach pupils to make constant reference to their spelling notebooks, the phonograms and the rules of spelling in the first seven pages of their notebook, to answer questions which arise. Each student's written work, reading and speech then reach constantly higher standards. He learns the patterns upon which our language forms words, and Anglicizes many foreign ones. This background can help him study any other alphabetic language.

The mental work habit of analyzing any new word into its phonograms and sounds is of high value in all his other studies. His writing of original sentences, paragraphs, stories and reports, together with his reading aloud from interesting well-written books and articles, does much to teach him the habit of good English grammar. He is able to read and then use words he has never seen or heard before, adding constantly from the beginning to his vocabulary.

This study of words and the use of them is the very basis upon which a student's advanced education in most other subjects depends.

Materials Needed for a Classroom
(*A summary of all materials recommended in this book*)

For the Teacher, 1 copy of this book including a recording of the phonogram sounds, 1 set of the 70 phonogram cards, 1 Morrison-McCall Spelling Scale pamphlet. (grades 2 to 13)

All classes need sets of books for their reading lessons. The books listed in the Appendix, page 276, suggest the kinds of books recommended. Open Court books are also recommended (see p. 285).

For each pupil, a six-sided, No. 2 pencil and lined writing paper. *For each pupil in Kindergarten and in Grade One,* 1 copy of the McCall-Harby Test Lessons in Primary Reading booklet. *For each pupil in Grade 2,* a copy of McCall-Crabbs Test Lessons in Reading, Booklet A. *For each pupil in 3rd Grade and above,* a copy of McCall-Crabbs Test Lessons in Reading, either booklet B, C, D or E depending on the age and achievement. *For each pupil in Kindergarten, Grade One and Grade Two,* a composition Notebook (see page 126). *For each pupil in Grade Three or above,* a larger composition Notebook (see page 127).

CHAPTER VI

TEACHING IN THE DIFFERENT GRADES

THE ABILITY, along with the desire, to read well-written books that expand the student's horizons and knowledge of life is one, if not the major, goal of language teaching. This interest should begin with the first book in Grade 1 and grow with the reading lessons in every subsequent grade.

Teach from the best written books at every level. Fine books fill the minds of children with a wealth of knowledge—of character and philosophy, of history and science, of humor and wit. Buying sets of these is not prohibitive if they can be shared by several classrooms and over a number of years by succeeding classes. (The total cost for learning handwriting, spelling and the reading of words is very little.)

Pupils take turns in reading aloud to the class without prior learning of new words. They meet, in fact, few new words to delay this reading if their spelling vocabulary has been taught a year ahead as is provided for in the spelling lessons. Through reading aloud pupils learn to speak and to write well also. This we owe *all* children.

The teacher need not ask detailed questions, which kill interest, about the content. Read Robert Frost's eight-line poem "The Pasture," for instance, and think how you would like to be asked insipid questions about it. Instead reread the poem to savor it because it produces such satisfying pictures in the mind's eye. Talking to some degree about the little calf and the pasture spring can add to the enchantment. Similarly, allusions can be made throughout the day to characters, phrases, or sentences encountered in books read or being read. In short, good books need to be savored for the beauty of the language and the sharing of the experiences of the characters portrayed. Essential questioning can be accomplished with the McCall-Harby booklets and the McCall-Crabbs Standard Test Lessons in Reading.

Books that have won the Newbery Award, or are good enough to win it, should be used for reading lessons. For too long children have been exposed to readers with highly controlled vocabularies, a practice that for many pupils is fatal to good writing and to interest in reading. Some beginning readers now are based on teaching phonics. Some of the worst are by linguists who offer the beginner sentences containing a repetition of the short sound of the letter a, for example, or, for the purpose of teaching, a sound of ow, etc. Such teaching belongs in the spelling lessons. From the beginning reading should be centered on the thought expressed by the author.

Children spend much time these days watching TV. This, like being read to, is no substitute for their class's reading aloud from good books—a process which, in addition to its other values, does much to unify the group. To keep the interest high collect all copies of a book being read after each day's lesson. When the written word is there for each child to see, time can be taken to appreciate the well-turned phrase, to admire or censure a happening, to read again a part that is especially worthy. In these ways children develop taste and become critical of the less good. Each child should always have a library book in his desk to read whenever time permits. His parents and he should be given a list of appropriate books to aid them in their selections.

The list of books to be found in the appendix to this volume is suggested for use in the reading lessons themselves. A sensitive children's librarian is invaluable in helping a teacher select books. The teacher who is confident that the books being read are worthwhile unconsciously conveys this confidence to the children.

Whole-Class Teaching

Teachers using the Spalding Method report that they find it an advantage to teach the whole class together. The only exception is the special attention given those having the most difficulty while the others do silent reading or writing. Teaching the whole group saves time and provides the pupils with the inspiration of learning and working together, but independently. Such teaching is most effective if the children are seated in separate, orderly rows of individual desks. All face the teacher. Any other seating lets pupils see and follow the writing of other pupils—and most often from a bad angle. This is harmful to those who have any difficulty in learning to write and read.

Whole-class teaching is a relief from the pressures of the competitive spirit which often prevails on the playground. There is a fascination for children in learning the basic tools of the written language. When these are well presented children soon acquire enough self-discipline to give full attention to the teacher.

With this kind of teaching the child becomes quiet, self-assured, respectful of his teacher, and the other children. He constantly competes with himself, trying to better his accomplishment, and accepts any suggestion for improvement gladly. If a child is pleased with his academic accomplishments but still shows personality problems, then the school must look elsewhere for the cause. However, if he is not doing well in speech, writing and reading, the school's first job is to teach him the basic techniques of language. A systematic, direct approach to his learning in school can show him how to attack other problems that beset him. This does not mean that the school should not help a child in whatever way it can, but such help should not be a *substitute* for teaching him.

"Handedness" (i.e., being left-handed or right-handed) or "eyedness" is not important if a child is correctly taught the language. What the child thinks he has said, seen, or heard is important. Left-handed children need have no more difficulty in learning than do others. The directions given on handwriting, except for the position of the paper and for slanting the connected writing, are the same as for the right-handed.

Pre-school Training

Teachers of four-year-olds in nursery school (and parents at home) can answer a child's questions on how one says, writes, or reads words by studying the previous chapters. Children want to write their names at age three, four, or five. They should be taught how to do so correctly, with a capital for the first letter and lower-case letters for the rest. They should be taught how to sit, how to hold the paper and pencil, and how to sound out. what they write. They come to school so that the teacher will *teach* them—not just to play or to express only what they already know.

Three-year-old children can learn to say the individual sounds of the phonogram cards, correlated with seeing the correct writing of the symbols. This gives a basis for correcting their speech as from "stan" to stand, "jist" to just, etc. Children at this age are eager to learn, and if they are correctly taught, the basis for a successful school life can be well laid.

Many kindergartens now teach writing and reading, and from the first day, and I recommend this. In general five-year-olds are less self-conscious about learning than are six-year-olds. They follow the Grade 1 program, but some groups go at a slower pace. Give extra help to those who write poorly to establish good motor patterns early, that they may go to Grade 1 without this handicap.

The First Grade

Three hours a day divided into suitable periods are needed for teaching the written language.

Learning to say the sounds of the seventy phonograms and learning to write correctly and legibly are two prerequisites to learning to spell and read.

A most important skill is correct pronunciation in clear, distinct speech during the spelling and reading lessons. The phonogram sounds in words are a direct aid in this. Clear speaking is not only good for its value in a direct phonics method. Everyone, unconsciously, judges any person by the quality of his speaking—some linguistics proponents notwithstanding. The teacher should help every child to correct any word he says in an incorrect or slovenly manner during his spelling or reading lessons. The accent marks on syllables have not been shown on the words in the Extended Ayres List. Teachers already know most of the accents in words and their effect on spellings or meanings. Teach the preferred pronunciation and in any doubtful case follow the information in the dictionary.

A good vocabulary is necessary for accurate thinking. A good written vocabulary is essential to logical, sequential reasoning. Learning these listed words by the Spalding Method makes it much easier for the student to enlarge his working vocabulary progressively.

The teaching of writing, as described in Chapter III, is combined with the teaching of the sounds of the phonograms from the start. The teacher uses the chalkboard as well as the phonogram cards and explains the applicable rules.

During the first week of October the teaching of at least thirty words a week is begun. The children write these words in their notebooks from the teacher's verbal dictation. Each day after the initial lesson, start with a written test, given by dictating the previous day's new words in a changed sequence. The test is on a separate paper and the child does not see his errors again. When a child misspells a word on his test paper, check this word in the child's notebook where the word is correctly written by him. He sees only his notebook, which he has corrected to agree with the teacher's writing on the chalkboard. (She makes sure his notebook is correct each time new words are put in it.) The checked words are his study lesson.

The mental habit to remember and to apply the simple rules about sounding and forming the letters is important. He must learn to think. The teacher must find time to help those who need extra teaching.

When the first book is presented to a class about November 1 it should be read as an adult reads his book. Discuss the author. The children have been writing what *they* say. They have by now read three or four sentences about one subject written on the board by the teacher. Similarly, the author of the book wanted to *talk* to the children, so he *wrote* in the book what he wanted to say. He has a name for his book. What does he call it?

Discuss how we talk, not by saying one word at a time, but by saying together the words which go together for the sense of the sentence. How far does the author's first idea go? Where is the first period on the page? That shows where the author's first idea ends. What does the author say in that sentence? Show that the word before a period at the end of a sentence never can be read with the word beginning the next sentence. A comma means that the word before it belongs there for its meaning. The word on the other side belongs there for its meaning. These two words may not be read together if the meaning of the sentence is to be clear. The sense of what is written is partially dependent on understanding the marks of punctuation.

Discuss the child's peripheral vision. Have each child hold his hands far out to the sides, look straight ahead and bring his hands in until he can see the tips of his fingers wiggle. He can see more than a yard across without turning his head. Therefore he can see the whole page at one glance since the page is not more than half a foot across. He can be led to *see* a sentence as a whole and thus read it as a complete thought (not word by word). He did this in reading his own sentences.

Reading first requires actual seeing. Children often insert or substitute their own words, or omit words, in reading. Reading aloud reveals this bad habit. The teacher must ask, "Did you really see what you have just read?" at every such error and have it read correctly. This teaches the important habit of seeing accurately.

Much reading aloud is needed to develop this habit of reading accurately. In reading we are trying to learn from the author and not to substitute our ideas for his.

Reading aloud can develop the habit of precise enunciation and improves both vocabulary and grammar. This practice in the skills of reading as well as learning to get the ideas from the printed page is essential. Correct meanings can only be learned from accurate reading. A knowledge of phonics is a prerequisite to accurate reading.

Each child in turn should be able to read the ideas presented in the sentences with easy expression. Words that do present a difficulty are sounded out as they are met. However, in reading *no* sounding out should be done aloud unless the child's silent sounding does not produce the correct word. Many teacher's manuals tell the teacher to present any new words to the class before they are met in the story to be read. They say that the one important thing is to get the meaning of the story. Children should get the meaning, of course, but their habits of mind should be considered too. They should work out the new words as they occur. No one is going to solve all their problems before each assignment when they are a little older. Telling pupils the new words fosters the mental habit which is seen in many children's inability to stick to an assignment, to concentrate in study periods, on homework, or on standardized tests. Children need to be taught ways of meeting problems as they arise and *not* to look for an escape.

If the method given in this book is taught, the child obtains in the spelling lesson the basic knowledge of how the written language works and he can figure out almost any word as he comes to it. If he needs some help, the teacher helps him only on the individual sound he does not recognize. He should expect to work out each word with the minimum of help. No other child should help him unless asked to do so by the teacher. Each child deserves to have the teacher teach him when he needs it.

If by February each year the children have studied the spelling words so as to make a score on the Morrison-McCall Spelling Scale (page 125) at least one year beyond their grade level, they will find few words in their reading that they cannot readily figure out and read.

The teacher's homework is, in part, to see that there are no words in the reading lesson for which she has no explanation as to how they work phonetically.

A successful first-grade teacher in teaching this method to her class of about fifty six-year-old children reported:

On the first day of school I showed the children how they should sit while writing, how to hold the pencil and how to use the "percolator," using the terminology of Mrs. Spalding. That term implies letting what they see or hear percolate (like water through the coffee) into their minds *before* they write or speak. The idea pleases them, and they get the point of thinking first, before acting. At the very beginning the habit of thinking, so necessary to success in learning, is being formed.

After that the single-letter cards are the order of the day. We review each day and add new ones. Provision is made for several periods each day. During these periods the children say the sounds and write on lined paper. One row at a time also writes on the chalkboard. In this way the formation of the letters and the ability of each child to learn are checked.

After two weeks most of the class is able to follow along as a group, and those who need extra help are singled out. When most of the children have a good idea of the single-letter sounds and their correct written forms (that is, they can write them from dictation and not from seeing the cards), we continue with the other phonograms, for they must know all the sounds *before* the words containing them are presented. The first fifty-four cards are necessary to write the words in the list to Section I. We begin writing the Extended Ayres List the first week in October.

I planned on thirty words a week and found it worked very well. The children sounded and wrote the thirty new words in their notebooks on Monday. We sounded out and then reread the first ten. These the children reviewed for homework. On Tuesday the children were given a twenty-word test, ten review words and the ten they had studied. On Tuesday the children studied and sounded the second column of ten. The test on Wednesday included columns 1 and 2. On Friday they were tested on the thirty words. In this way those who were absent for a day or two were able to cover the material they had missed. It also helped the children who needed review. I found when I began to review words through Section L in February that the children had really grasped them.

The children started reading books on November 1 and they were then well past Section I in the spelling list. At the beginning I divided the class into two groups, 36 in my first group and 18 in my second. This enabled me to give those who needed less teaching a good start and to get them to work independently in answering written questions on the stories they read. In reading, one group in the room never read aloud a story already read aloud by another group. In this way each child has an opportunity to show he can read independently. All can do this. Many have read many library books during the year and have, because of it, much more expression and fluency. However, *all* can read and *all* comprehend.

At the beginning of February we started to review. Each day the children wrote on separate sheets five words from Sections A–H and ten words from Sections I to M (all review) and put five new words from M and the following sections in their notebooks. These new words were sounded by the children individually as they wrote them, then were read without being sounded out, and finally used in a sentence. Tests were given each day. The words spelled incorrectly were checked in their notebooks and the per cent of errors written on the top of the page. In this way both children and parents could note progress and review, now and again, those words not mastered. By June we reached Section O.

The children composed and wrote their own sentences as soon as they started Section H. In this way they learned to use a capital where they should and also to use a period or question mark at the end of each sentence. They like to illustrate their sentences in original art, which requires more thought about the meaning of words.

Forty-two different trade books were read aloud before June by this first-grade class in their reading lessons.

This teacher held a series of after-school classes for parents. She taught them this method and they became a very real help, especially to the children who needed it most.

Test Lessons in Primary Reading by McCall-Harby reprinted by the Spalding Education Foundation are fine for teaching children to answer written questions about what they have read. Ten questions answered by yes or no are asked about each of the thirty paragraphs.

Second Grade

If the class has not been taught the Spalding method in the first grade, it is necessary to give them the entire first-grade work before going further, but this can be done more rapidly than with a first-grade group of children.

For classes who need only review, this can be done in the first few weeks. The teacher dictates about 100 words a day from the Extended Ayres List and the children write them on separate sheets as a test. Those missed are taught as in Chapter V and put in the notebooks.

This and constant testing and review should be carried on until the class has learned to write correctly the words through Section Q in the Extended Ayres List. They find few words which are not already in their understanding and speaking vocabulary.

Point out every neglect of any of the rules of pronunciation, of writing, or of spelling which each child's work evidences, and require him to state the rule and make the correction himself in all his lessons.

The list of books given in the appendix indicates the literary quality of books to be read aloud in the reading lessons. The teacher brings background information and explains word meanings so that all children—not just those who will read on their own—experience the reading of stories of book length. Too much reading in school is in little pieces. However, short stories are good if they have literary value.

Second-graders learn cursive writing after Christmas. They say the sounds of the letters in the order in which they appear in the alphabet and learn to connect the manuscript alphabet. (See page 83.) Teach them to sound and to learn to write the seventy phonograms in cursive writing. They then write the Extended Ayres List in cursive writing. Once cursive writing is introduced do no more manuscript writing except for maps and posters. When the list is dictated this time add endings appropriate to some of the base words. Dictate the base word and then that word with any common ending: last, lasts, lasted, lasting; old, older, oldest; train, trains, trained, training, trainer, etc. This the pupils can then do in study periods with the words of subsequent lessons.

Use the McCall-Crabbs Standard Test Lessons in Reading—Book B to teach children to hold their minds on what they read. With practice they can answer the eight to ten questions about a paragraph without looking back to find many answers. Use half the book for teaching this. Use the next paragraphs as timed tests which show the grade placement. Averaging the scores on ten paragraphs gives a good indication of comprehension.

Have a time each day when every child writes a short paragraph on a subject of his choosing. Part of his homework is to find a subject. Children who are reading good books reflect this in their writing and in their reading of them aloud. The slovenly speech now so prevalent can be fully corrected in the second grade.

Third Grade

The third grade starts with a complete review of the first- and second-grade work. The pupils write for the first time the seven pages of the Notebook in their notebooks for reference. Each child also enters in his notebook the words, through Section Q, which he misses in the review of the first- and second-grade words from the Extended

Ayres List. This is his individual list. Dictate all the words beginning with Section R. The pupils write all these words in the notebooks. Continue to repeat the spelling rules, the elements for correct posture and good writing habits. Correct the pronunciation of words and the sounds and writing of phonograms.

Those children in the class who may not have had this method in the previous grade need to start at the beginning and proceed more slowly at first unless they learn rapidly during the review period at the start of the term. Many schools use a summer session for this purpose.

It is advisable to seat such children and any others who have difficulty near the front where the teacher can supervise and guide them more easily. Let the other children go ahead with reading to themselves and with other such work during the times when the teacher is working with the smaller group of children who need to learn spelling commensurate with their grade. All third-graders should learn the words at least to Section X. For most of the class there will be time to go through all the rest of the words in the Extended Ayres List.

It is in the third grade that children find the use of the dictionary even more valuable. They discover the many prefixes and endings for base words as well as the synonyms, and see how the spelling rules for endings apply. They become more interested in meanings and where words come from—especially those that do not follow common English patterns.

The daily writing of compositions should be continued. They now can be based on the history, science and literature the class has studied. Have as many children as possible write at the chalkboard. The others write at their desks. Then the chalkboard paragraphs are read aloud and any errors discussed and corrected. Those at the desks, having observed the chalkboard errors, then correct their own papers before the teacher corrects them. This grade is where the benefits from having read more advanced books of quality on history, science and similar subjects are reflected in the children's compositions.

Book C of the Standard Test Lessons in Reading is good for training and testing in comprehension in third grade.

Fourth and Higher Grades

Each class reviews and writes again the first seven pages of the Notebook and is tested on the Extended Ayres List from the beginning. Any words which a child misses in the initial review he puts in his notebook and the teacher finds time to dictate these to him as soon as possible. This shows the teacher where each child and the whole class needs teaching. All children put all the words beyond Section X in their notebooks. When this is done, we shall not be sending children with second-grade spelling ability on to higher grades. The elementary school is charged with the teaching of the elements of the language. It is remiss unless it provides the *time* and the *teaching* which accomplish this for each child.

When pupils ask for the spelling of words they do not know, the teacher asks the pupil to sound the word and she corrects any inaccurate sounds. He writes the parts of the word he can and the teacher helps only with those parts he does not know. From third grade on the dictionary should be used when the teacher is not readily available.

Speed reading, which is currently being widely taught, is suitable only for children who have really learned to read; that is, to read accurately. It is no substitute for the basic teaching of the language subjects. Time spent speeding up inaccuracies is wasteful.

The McCall-Crabbs Standard Test Lessons in Reading, Books C, D and E, are fine for the fourth and higher grades. They let the child and the teacher know how he stands in comprehension just as the Morrison-McCall Spelling Scale tests used each month show constantly the teacher's effectiveness in the teaching of spelling.

Sixth-grade students need teaching in basic grammar to be able to analyze and identify the grammatical parts of almost any sentence. This may or may not require a textbook grammar, as the teacher prefers. The understanding of grammar aids the pupils' ability to write. Basic grammar was started in Grade 1.

The early advanced mastery of English writing and reading under this method enabled my sixth-grade class of thirty-two at the Bronxville Public School to read together six excellent story books on the Middle Ages. We purchased enough copies, and the pupils took turns in reading aloud from them. We learned how people of the time made ink, wrote and illuminated and bound their books, and wove their tapestries, and then we practiced these same skills. When we thereafter visited museums to view their collections, the class gained a real appreciation of that part of our cultural heritage. It was a part of their history lesson. I mention this to indicate how a teacher can provide this sort of background knowledge in order to make reading come alive. Many read about fifty books on the subject.

Classes in adult education find the use of the Spalding Method successful. Foreigners studying English quickly acquire a grasp of our language if it is presented by this method. Without this logical approach English is one of the most difficult languages for them. Teachers also are now using it with geat success in Japan, the Philippines and Hong Kong. This book has been translated into Japanese by Professor Furu Hashi and Assistant Professor Momoyo Fukada at the Toyota College of Technology.

The need for remedial-reading teaching should be minimal if classroom teachers follow this method well. Where tutoring is necessary it can be effected in a minimum of time. When I have taught individual children who were having difficulty in the language subjects, I have required the parents of children of elementary-school age especially to work with the children and me through the lessons so that they can help the youngsters at home. This can make for a strong bond between child and parent. When a parent does not know how to help, he is placed in the unhappy role of a taskmaster. There is much untapped assistance for the teacher in the parents of the children who need more help.

Special classes for children with learning disabilities and also classes for educable retarded children have made great gains by using this method.

High-school students who have not been taught by this method can benefit greatly from it as the following quotation from a teacher's report indicates:

After two months' work last fall with my five senior English classes, I realized that the students were not able to go ahead with a regular 12th grade curriculum without special assistance from somewhere. They misspelled simple words. Most of them approached English and reading as though it were impossible of comprehension by any normal being.

The teaching of Old and Middle English literature to people who could not read present-day English was highly improbable and I found the students blithely flunking exams with grades of 10 and 20 rather than attempting to do the homework connected with literature.

Some of them could quote grammar rules, name parts of speech and even diagram sentences with easy fluency but they could not write. I found I could not teach composition because they did not have the tools for self-expression.

Vocabulary was just as hopeless. They reacted with resentment when they found that there were shades of meaning for the correct usage of a word.

The first spelling tests I gave showed the same incomprehension. After the first two letters, a word, to most of them, was simply a wild jumble of letters which carried no meaning either to their eyes or their ears.

The result was that I stopped all regular work in English and started the students out on a six-weeks' course of Mrs. Spalding's method. We made notebooks, using the first seven pages as a graphic presentation of the rules of spelling. Then we started on the lists of spelling words which commenced with Sections A–H.

Although they started the new regime somewhat rebelliously, the students soon recognized that the sounding of the letters was not only teaching them spelling, but correct speech sounds without the embarrassment of working in front of a group. As they began to comprehend the letters by sound, the English language began to fall into order in their minds and they began to find that they had a whole new grasp of their own language. This was apparent to me in the growing unity and cooperation in the classes. For the first time I was not pulling against them.

Soon students began coming to my desk and expressing appreciation of the work I was giving them, telling me that they had never been taught like that before. One boy told me, "If I could spell, I could learn to read!"

The results of the first spelling test showed that the average grade level of these senior high school students was between sixth- and seventh-grade. If I had given the first test before we started on Mrs. Spalding's regime, the average would have been probably at fifth grade. On the second test, given a month later, the average rose about half a grade level. But the mistakes consisted of only one letter in a three-, four-, or five-syllable word. The average of the class in spelling has risen steadily until time for their college entrance examinations.

About one-third of the whole senior class has taken the college entrance examinations (the highest number yet to do so in the history of the school).

The good students have become much more secure; the poor students are by now passing in their twelfth-grade work. None of this would have been possible if I had not been able to give the students a grounding in the English language. During the first two months I was failing with them, as other teachers before me had failed. And I would still be failing if I had not had this concise, logical and most readily teachable method to present to my classes. Giving my students this work has solved not only their most obvious problems in speech and the use of English but also the more subtle problems of courtesy and class behavior. I simply do not have the disciplinary problems that bedevil so many of my colleagues.

This book is a textbook for teachers of the basic elements of

English, but it may be of interest and helpful to quote from the comments by a principal of a large school (kindergarten through eighth grade) after seven years' experience with the Spalding Method in all her classrooms, and also from a letter by the superintendent of twenty-four Hawaiian schools where it has been long in use.

The principal wrote:

Bright children go forward at an amazing pace into the world of books. The method does its work surely and quickly for this type of child. Their independence in attacking new words and their freedom from the slavery of remembering the countless words of our language stimulate their desire to achieve . . .

Slower children are none the less benefited. These children go through a similar development but at their own rate of achievement. The method is ideally geared to the individuality of the child, to his slower learning ability.

He masters a definite number of phonograms at his own pace. The emotional upset and frustration of trying to recall hundreds of sight words is avoided. The seeing, saying and writing of the sounds almost simultaneously eliminates some of the slow child's biggest reading pitfalls, such as reversals, poor auditory discrimination, inability to follow directions, and general habits of inattention.

I have dwelt at length on the beginnings, but here, as in every worthwhile undertaking, beginnings count double. Our beginnings, thanks to the Unified Phonic Method approach to the Language Arts, have counted for double or more. We have a small quota of slow readers, but not one non-reader. Our slow readers are in fact a definite proof of the genuineness and completeness reliability of the method. These readers are slow, but they are *always progressing.* Our classroom records show steady, even daily reading progress for all our children of low average or very low mental ability.

An overall proof of the excellent results of using this method over a period of seven years is the reading consciousness throughout the school and the consistent scholastic achievement. Because the pupils can read, teachers have been able to take the time to guide them into important phases of comprehension and into the intellectual wealth of the literature of the language. Reading can be directed, individualized, and made the gateway to knowledge and wisdom.

The Spalding method requires from the teacher dedication and hard work. If a teacher is seeking an easy way of teaching, let her look elsewhere—it is not here. If she is seeking a sure way, let her look into this method with an open mind and a real desire to know. If she is seeking a way to guide children through reading to well adjusted personality, this method will not fail her.

Through the use of this method in our school we have had the satisfaction of seeing very large classes of children well started in reading, adventuring on their own and achieving in general scholastic work. In fine we have experienced the joy of a difficult task well done.

The superintendent expressed his attitude toward this method:

This approach to the comprehensive mastery of language is the only logical one. It comes to grips immediately with the symbolic character of the spoken and written word and shows the inter-relationship of the two symbol systems and their power to evoke common meanings.

Pupils, too, are quick to feel a sense of satisfaction in the "workableness" of the approach. They gain a healthy independence from the teacher and all extrinsic aids. Once the tools of learning are mastered the way to learning lies open. If some children seem to master the tools of language effortlessly and without the need for method, still many do not. Furthermore, it cannot be denied that whatever the ability of the pupil, this is a systematic and scientific way to lead him to language facility.

The *early* mastery of a good vocabulary for both writing and reading becomes more urgent every year. Until that is learned it is almost impossible to teach even a rudimentary understanding of the rapidly changing scientific and mechanical world with which we now have to cope. So much more must be learned that the time of the child and of the teacher is ever more precious. The Spalding Method of teaching the basic language subjects directly by phonics and the spelling rules greatly expedites the time when every child in school becomes competent to learn other advanced subjects.

Notes—

1. In this book I have referred to the original 1965 McCall-Harby and the 1961 McCall-Crabbs Test Lessons in Reading. These have now been reprinted and are available through the Spalding Education Foundation, 15410 N. 67th Ave., Suite 8, Glendale, AZ 85306.

CHAPTER VII

ADVANCING BASIC EDUCATION

IT HAS BEEN our one objective in this book to provide teachers, educators and parents (and our children) with the most effective access to the rapid mastery of the basic elements of English, a facility which is urgently, directly and currently needed. Others have exposed the serious failures of current methods of teaching accurate reading, clear writing and speaking. These skills are absolute prerequisites to the study of history, literature, science and most other subjects in education, including much of mathematics. This is a scientific age which has amassed so much new knowledge in so short a period that children need all possible time to acquire even enough rudimentary knowledge of the modern world we live in, and its rapid changes, to form valid judgments about the problems it creates. The first years in school are the most receptive ones for acquiring rapidly the basic elements of English, and this permits early study in the other fields of education, where understanding of the laws of nature helps develop the student's reasoning faculty. This latter is a major goal in education. It relies on a fund of knowledge and an extensive vocabulary with which to think and to express one's thoughts on paper and orally.

The communication gap, which blocks understandings everywhere in recent days, is little more than the inability of many men to express themselves clearly in English. For that is the international language most used to negotiate problems between nations, between races, between labor and management—between all diverse groups in America. The accurate, clear use of spoken and written English can go far to cause reason and understanding to prevail over the prejudice, emotions and pride that so often lead to violence and war.

It is said that man learns from his past mistakes and advances his civilization chiefly because he has been able to transmit in writing the knowledge and the thinking of the minds of many past generations. Everyone is born a helpless, self-centered child who must be taught to restrain many of his instincts, to regard the rights and feelings of others, and to communicate. When he begins to write and read and to do work with his mind he needs the right guidance to attain his full potential. The need for the earliest practical teaching of these skills to all children was never more apparent. Good employment is fast becoming impossible for those who cannot read and write accurately. Failure in these skills leads directly to much of the poverty, delinquency, illiteracy and violent revolts in the cities. All studies of these problems agree that better education is the primary remedy.

The purpose of this new edition is not to alter the well-proved Spalding Method but to make more fully and clearly available (all within these pages) the method of improving the teaching of the fundamentals of education, namely the speaking, writing and reading of English. These are only the essential tools of education to which every child is entitled in order that he may develop his maximum inherent mental and spiritual abilities. Many other things are needed to bring forth the best in a man, but without these basic tools of language at his command he cannot realize his natural capabilities. Many fine minds are denied their full growth and contributions to mankind because they lack these basic means of communication from others (as in reading) and with others (as in speaking and writing).

It has been my privilege, after having been a classroom teacher in all the elementary grades, to teach my method to over two hundred classes averaging forty teachers and parents during vacation periods in some twenty states and Canada. I have found that a forty-hour course was best to prepare a teacher properly to teach this method to her class, and I recommend *that* much study of this book to anyone about to teach from it. I have not known any teacher who, once she has taught this method, willingly changed to another. Its value is also attested to by the continued demand for the book during the years since it was first published in 1957. A large volume of statistical standard test scores from public and private schools from many areas have been sent to me. However, much background data are needed to judge these tests. It may suffice to state that all these median scores show considerable gains above the United States norms for the various student tests in both reading and spelling in every grade. Teachers value the logic of the method and its directness.

The question may arise as to whether it is necessary to teach pupils to write, by analysis of the sounds, some 1700 words and to say the sounds as they write, in order to learn and master that many. These words are but a small number of the English words which an educated person will need to know and use in the modern world, but they do cover practically every pattern of English spelling and speaking. The point is that the work of mastering the basic elements of these words has taught the pupil the phonics of English and the spelling rules so thoroughly that he is able to decipher quickly almost any new English word he may read or hear. He has learned the necessary tools for a basic mastery of English words, and his writing and reading will have taught him the habit of using good grammar, sentence structure and style.

It can be useful here to summarize briefly the salient features of the Spalding method:

The pupils listen to the whole word dictated by the teacher. They then each say each component phonogram sound, or syllable, in it, just before they write each one, and then read aloud the word from their own writing. This mental work of writing the symbols (phonograms) of the sounds heard in the word, and also of applying any spelling rules which may affect it, greatly reduces the number of silent letters that need be memorized for correctly writing it, or for accurately saying it, or for quickly recognizing it in print. The early habit of using one's knowledge of phonics and the spelling rules to derive the sounds in a printed word, or to write a spoken word, develops the mental habit of thinking to read any new printed word, and of using the more accurate words to express one's idea in speaking or writing. This working use of the mind, free from sole reliance on one's visual memory, promotes true education.

A further major advantage of the Spalding Method is that its continuous combining of the pupils' hearing, saying, writing and seeing in the teaching of words prevents the tendency of so many beginners to develop frustrating dyslexia. It is also considered the most effective method of overcoming much of this handicap after serious dyslexia has already taken hold.

No exposure to devices that show or sound the component parts heard in a word can teach a word half as well and as quickly as does the work done by the pupil in producing it himself. It is the mental work of using the mind to control the voice muscles in saying, and the hand in writing, the component parts heard in a word which best teaches that word.

One of our objectives in writing this book is to help prevent the unhappiness and the appalling loss resulting from so large a proportion of the population living and thinking, working and producing, at levels far below their inborn mental abilities because of their relative inability to write and read. We also have reason to hope that this book and the method it teaches will lead to a genuine upgrading of the standards of scholarship and educational objectives in our schools and colleges. We believe that this book presents one indispensable, basic step toward these important goals.

APPENDIX

LIST OF SELECTED BOOKS by Grades (which of course overlap) Suggested for Purchase in Sets, for Pupils Reading Aloud in Class for the Reading Lessons.

Books for Kindergarten and Grade One

PAPERBACK

Random House, Beginner Book Series
(Read these five books in the order listed after completing the writing of the spelling words to Section I.)

Ten Apples up on Top
Green Eggs and Ham
Go, Dog, Go
Put Me in the Zoo
Are You My Mother?

Scholastic Book Services
(After writing the words to Section L, books from this list can be read. Continuing to Section O makes it possible to read all of them.)

The Carrot Seed
Curious George
Madeline
The Biggest Bear

The Five Chinese Brothers
The Story of Ferdinand
The Story of Ping

The Economy Company
Pelle's New Suit
Sam's First Fish
The Gingerbread Boy
The Outside Cat
The Three Bears and Goldilocks
The Three Billy Goats Gruff
The Three Little Pigs

Grolier Inc., The Beginning Reader's Program
Johnny Crow's Garden, illus. by Leslie Brooke
The House That Jack Built, illus. by Randolph Caldecott
The Mother Goose Treasury, illus. by Kate Greenaway
The Tale of Peter Rabbit, from the original publication

TRADE BOOKS
(Many of these titles are now available in paperback.)

ANDERSON, C. W.	*Billy and Blaze*	Macmillan
BEMELMANS, LUDWIG	*Madeline's Rescue*	Viking
BROWN, MARCIA	*Dick Whittington and His Cat*	Scribner
BROWN, MARCIA	*Once a Mouse*	Scribner
BURTON, VIRGINIA	*Mike Mulligan and His Steam Shovel*	Houghton
CALHOUN, MARY	*Cross-Country Cat*	Morrow
DE REGNIERS, BEATRICE	*May I Bring a Friend?*	Atheneum
DOUGHERTY, JAMES	*Andy and the Lion*	Viking
ETS, MARIE	*Just Me*	Viking
FIELD, RACHEL	*Prayer for a Child*	Macmillan
FLACK, MARJORIE	*Angus and the Ducks*	Doubleday
FLACK, MARJORIE	*Wait for William*	Houghton
GAG, WANDA	*Millions of Cats*	Coward

GEISEL, T. S.	*And to Think I Saw It on Mulberry Street*	Vanguard
GRIMM, JACOB	*The Wolf and the Seven Kids*	Harcourt
GRAMATKY, HARDIE	*Little Toot on the Thames*	Putnam
HADER, B. AND E.	*The Big Snow*	Macmillan
HADER, B. AND E.	*Little Appaloosa*	Macmillan
HOFF, SYD	*Sammy the Seal*	Harper
HUTCHINS, PAT	*The Very Worst Monster*	Greenwillow
KEATS, EZRA	*Whistle for Willie*	Viking
LAMORISSE, ALBERT	*The Red Balloon*	Doubleday
LEFEVRE, FELICITE	*The Cock, the Mouse and the Little Red Hen*	Macrae
LIONNI, LEO	*Frederick*	Obolensky
LIONNI, LEO	*Inch by Inch*	Obolensky
McCLOSKEY, ROBERT	*Blueberries for Sal*	Viking
McCLOSKEY, ROBERT	*Make Way for Ducklings*	Viking
McCLOSKEY, ROBERT	*One Morning in Maine*	Viking
MINARIK, ELSE	*Little Bear*	Harper
PARISH, PEGGY	*Amelia Bedelia series*	Greenwillow
PETERSHAM, MAUD	*The Rooster Crows*	Macmillan
PERRAULT, CHARLES	*Cinderella*	Scribner
PIPER, WATTY	*The Little Engine That Could*	Platt
SENDAK, MAURICE	*Where the Wild Things Are*	Harper
SHEEHAN, ANGELA	*My First Book of Nature: The Mouse*	Warwick
ZIM, HERBERT	*Rabbits*	Morrow

Grade Two

AESOP	*The Hare and the Tortoise*	McGraw

ANDERSEN, HANS C.	*The Emperor's New Clothes*	Houghton
ANDERSEN, HANS C.	*The Steadfast Tin Soldier*	Scribner
ANGLUND, JOAN	*Brave Cowboy*	Harcourt
ANGLUND, JOAN	*Christmas Is a Time of Giving*	Harcourt
ANGLUND, JOAN	*In a Pumpkin Shell*	Harcourt
ANGLUND, JOAN	*Love Is a Special Way of Feeling*	Harcourt
ANGLUND, JOAN	*Nibble, Nibble, Mousekin*	Harcourt
ANGLUND, JOAN	*Spring Is a New Beginning*	Harcourt
BONTEMPS, ARNA	*The Fast Sooner Hound*	Houghton
CARLSON, NATALIE	*The Family Under the Bridge*	Harper
CLEARY, BEVERLY	*The Mouse on the Motorcycle*	Morrow
COLE, JOANNA	*A Frog's Body* (and other books in *Body* series)	Morrow
DALGLIESH, ALICE	*The Bears on Hemlock Mountain*	Scribner
GOUDEY, ALICE	*Houses from the Sea*	Scribner
HANDFORTH, THOMAS	*Mei Li*	Doubleday
LOVELACE, MAUDE H., BETSY AND JOE	*Betsy-Tacy series*	Harper
MCCLOSKEY, ROBERT	*Time of Wonder*	Viking
MERRIAM, EVE	*Blackberry Ink*	Morrow
MILNE, A. A.	*The World of Christopher Robin*	Dutton
POLITI, LEO	*Mr. Fong's Toy Shop*	Scribner
POLITI, LEO	*Song of Swallows*	Scribner
PRELUTSKY, JACK	*The New Kid on the Block*	Greenwillow
SIMON, SEYMOUR	*Saturn*	Morrow
SIMON, SEYMOUR	*Jupiter*	Morrow

| THURBER, JAMES | *Many Moons* | Harcourt |
| WILLIAMS, MARGERY | *The Velveteen Rabbit* | Doubleday |

Grade Three

ALEXANDER, BEATRICE	*Famous Myths of the Golden Age*	Random
ATWATER, RICHARD	*Mr. Popper's Penguins*	Little
BLEEKER, SONIA	*The Cherokee Indians*	Morrow
BLEEKER, SONIA	*The Chippewa*	Morrow
BLEEKER, SONIA	*The Delaware*	Morrow
BLEEKER, SONIA	*The Sioux*	Morrow
BLUME, JUDY	*Freckle Juice*	Four Winds
BUFF, MARY	*Dancing Cloud* (Navajo)	Viking
BUTTERWORTH, OLIVER	*The Enormous Egg*	Little
CLARK, ANN	*In My Mother's House* (Pueblo)	Viking
CLEARY, BEVERLY	*Henry Huggins* (and other *Henry* titles)	Morrow
CLEARY, BEVERLY	*Ramona the Pest* (and other *Ramona* titles)	Morrow
COATSWORTH, ELIZABETH	*The Cat Who Went to Heaven*	Macmillan
D'AULAIRE, I. AND E.	*Abraham Lincoln*	Doubleday
D'AULAIRE, I. AND E.	*Benjamin Franklin*	Doubleday
D'AULAIRE, I. AND E.	*Columbus*	Doubleday
D'AULAIRE, I. AND E.	*George Washington*	Doubleday
D'AULAIRE, I. AND E.	*Leif the Lucky*	Doubleday
D'AULAIRE, I. AND E.	*Pocahontas*	Doubleday
DALGLIESH, ALICE	*Bears on Hemlock Mountain*	Scribner
DALGLIESH, ALICE	*Fourth of July Story*	Scribner
DALGLIESH, ALICE	*The Courage of Sarah Noble*	Scribner

DALGLIESH, ALICE	*The Thanksgiving Story*	Scribner
DE ANGELI, MAR- GUERITE	*Door in the Wall*	Doubleday
DE ANGELI, MAR- GUERITE	*Thee, Hannah!*	Doubleday
HOLLING, H. C.	*Paddle to the Sea*	Houghton
HURWITZ, JOHANNA	*Aldo Applesauce*	Morrow
KIPLING, RUDYARD	*Just So Stories*	Doubleday
LAWSON, PETER	*Rabbit Hill*	Viking
LAWSON, ROBERT	*Ben and Me*	Little
PETERSHAM, MAUD	*The Silver Mace*	Macmillan
SASEK, M.	*This Is Greece*	Macmillan
SASEK, M.	*This Is London*	Macmillan
WHITE, E. B.	*Charlotte's Web*	Harper
ZIM, HERBERT	*Dinosaurs*	Morrow
ZIM, HERBERT	*Little Cats*	Morrow
ZIM, HERBERT	*Owls*	Morrow
ZIM, HERBERT	*Rabbits*	Morrow
ZIM, HERBERT	*Snakes*	Morrow

Grade Four

AESOP	*The Fables of Aesop*	Macmillan
ALCOTT, LOUISA	*Little Women*	Dutton
AVERILL, ESTHER	*Cartier Sails the St. Lawrence*	Harper
BLEEKER, SONIA	*The Apache Indians*	Morrow
BLEEKER, SONIA	*The Sioux Indians*	Morrow
CARROLL, LEWIS	*Alice's Adventures in Wonderland*	Macmillan
COLUM, PADRAIC	*The Children's Homer*	Macmillan
D'AULAIRE, I. AND E.	*Book of Greek Myths*	Doubleday
D'AULAIRE, I. AND E.	*Norse Gods and Giants*	Doubleday
D'AULAIRE, I. AND E.	*Pocahontas*	Doubleday
DAUGHERTY, JAMES	*Andy and the Lion*	Viking

DEJONG, MEINDERT	*The House of Sixty Fathers*	Harper
DODGE, MARY	*Hans Brinker*	Scribner
EDMONDS, WALTER	*The Matchlock Gun*	Dodd
ESTES, ELEANOR	*Ginger Pye*	Harcourt
FADIMAN, CLIFTON	*The Adventures of Hercules*	Random
FORBES, ESTHER	*America's Paul Revere*	Houghton
GANNETT, RUTH	*My Father's Dragon*	Random
GILSON, JAMIE	*Thirteen Ways to Sink a Sub*	Lothrop, Lee & Shepard
GRIMM, JACOB	*Household Stories of the Brothers Grimm*	Dover
GRIMM, JACOB	*Grimm's Fairy Tales* (illus. by Ellison and Adams)	Routledge & Kegan
HENRY, MARGUERITE	*Benjamin West and His Cat Grimlakin*	Bobbs
LENSKI, LOIS	*Prairie School*	Lippincott
LEWELLEN, JOHN	*Moon, Sun and Stars*	Children's
SYME, ROLAND	*First Around the World*	Morrow
TRAVERS, P. L.	*Mary Poppins* (rev. ed.)	Harcourt
TRAVERS, P. L.	*Mary Poppins in Cherry Tree Lane*	Delacorte, Dell
TRAVERS, P. L.	*Mary Poppins in the Park*	Harcourt
TRAVERS, P. L.	*Mary Poppins Opens the Door*	Harcourt
TRAVERS, P. L.	*Mary Poppins Comes Back*	Harcourt
WHITE, E. B.	*Stuart Little*	Harper
WILDER, LAURA	*Farmer Boy*	Harper
WILDER, LAURA	*Little House in the Big Wood*	Harper

WILDER, LAURA	*On the Banks of Plum Creek*	Harper
ZIM, HERBERT	*Rabbits*	Morrow
ZIM, HERBERT	*World of Sharks*	Morrow
ZIM, HERBERT	*The Universe*	Morrow
ZIM, HERBERT	*Your Skin*	Morrow

Grade Five

ALCOTT, LOUISA	*Little Men*	Little
BENNETT, JOHN	*Master Skylark*	Grosset
BRINK, CAROL	*Caddie Woodlawn*	Macmillan
CARSON, RACHEL	*The Sea Around Us*	Simon
CLEARY, BEVERLY	*Dear Mr. Henshaw*	Morrow
COLUM, PADRAIC	*The Children of Odin*	Macmillan
DAUGHERTY, JAMES	*Landing of the Pilgrims*	Random
DE ANGELI, MARGUERITE	*Door in the Wall*	Doubleday
DEFOE, DANIEL	*Robinson Crusoe*	Lippincott
DEJONG, MEINDERT	*The Wheel on the School*	Harper
DU BOIS, W. P.	*The Twenty-one Balloons*	Viking
EATON, JEANETTE	*Lone Journey*	Harcourt
FOSTER, GENEVIEVE	*George Washington's World*	Scribner
GATES, DORIS	*Blue Willow*	Viking
GEORGE, JEAN	*My Side of the Mountain*	Dutton
GRAHAME, KENNETH	*Wind in the Willows*	Scribner
LANG, ANDREW	*Arabian Nights*	Longmans
LATHAM, JEAN	*Carry On, Mr. Bowditch*	Houghton
MCNEER, MAY	*The Hudson: River of History*	Garrard

MORRIS, RICHARD	*American Revolution*	Lerner
MORRIS, RICHARD	*The Constitution* (rev. ed.)	Lerner
MORRIS, RICHARD	*The Founding of the Republic*	Lerner
SEREDY, KATE	*The Good Master*	Viking
SEREDY, KATE	*White Stag*	Viking Penguin
SPERRY, ARMSTRONG	*Call It Courage*	Macmillan

Grade Six

BENARY-ISBERT	*Blue Mystery*	Harcourt
BULFINCH, THOMAS	*A Book of Myths*	Macmillan
COLUM, PADRAIC	*The Golden Fleece and the Heroes Before*	Macmillan
COMMAGER, HENRY S.	*Great Constitution*	Bobbs
COY, HAROLD	*The First Book of the Supreme Court*	Watts
CRISMAN, ARTHUR	*Shen of the Sea*	Dutton
DAUGHERTY, JAMES	*Landing of the Pilgrims*	Random
DOORLY	*Insect Man*	Dufour
FARJEON, ELEANOR	*Glass Slipper*	Ace Books
FIELD, RACHEL	*Hitty: Her First Hundred Years*	Macmillan
FOSTER, GENEVIEVE	*George Washington's World*	Scribner
FOSTER, GENEVIEVE	*Abraham Lincoln's World*	Scribner
FOSTER, GENEVIEVE	*Year of Columbus, 1492*	Scribner
FOSTER, GENEVIEVE	*Year of the Horseless Carriage*	Scribner
GRAY, ELIZABETH	*Adam of the Road*	Viking
HARTMAN, GERTRUDE	*Medieval Days and Ways*	Macmillan
ISH-KISHOR, S.	*Our Eddie*	Pantheon
KELLY, ERIC	*The Trumpeteer of Krakow*	Macmillan

KRUMGOLD, JOSEPH	*Onion John*	Crowell
L'ENGLE, MADELEINE	*A Wrinkle in Time*	Farrar
MALORY, SIR THOMAS	*The Boy's King Arthur*	Scribner
PYLE, HOWARD	*Men of Iron*	Harper
RAWLINGS, MARJORIE	*The Yearling*	Scribner
SANDBURG, CARL	*Abe Lincoln Grows Up*	Harcourt
SHIPPEN, KATHERINE	*Graham Bell Invents the Telephone*	Random
SPEARE, ELIZABETH	*The Bronze Bow*	Houghton
SEREDY, KATE	*The White Stag*	Viking
STEVENSON, ROBERT L.	*Treasure Island*	Macmillan
SUTCLIFF, ROSEMARY	*Frontier Wolf*	Dutton
SUTCLIFF, ROSEMARY	*Light Beyond the Forest*	Dutton
SUTCLIFF, ROSEMARY	*Road to Camlaan*	Dutton
SUTCLIFF, ROSEMARY	*Simon*	Oxford University Press
SUTCLIFF, ROSEMARY	*Sword and the Circle*	Dutton
WHITE, ANNE TERRY	*Lost Worlds*	Random
WILDER, LAURA	*Little Town on the Prairie and Other Titles*	Harper
VAN LOON, HENDRIK	*Story of Mankind*	Liveright
YATES, ELIZABETH	*Amos Fortune, Free Man*	Dutton
ZIM AND BAKER	*Stars*	Golden

If sets of readers are desired, Open Court Publishing Co., P.O. Box 599, La Salle, Illinois 61301, has classic stories which should be read without introducing new words. Open Court Rise readers are available for grades four through six.

Poetry books have not been listed beyond the second grade. A set of a selected anthology to be shared by third through sixth grades should be considered. Desired poems are often found only in volumes written by individual poets. Children learn poems so easily. The best of our heritage should be read by them and many memorized. They will be a source of pleasure all their lives.

The American Association for the Advancement of Science at 1333 H Street, N.W., Washington, D.C. 20005 has a book list for children of elementary-school age. The Metropolitan Museum of Art, New York, N.Y., has a list of art books recommended for children of five to fourteen years of age.

Your public library should have a list of Newbery and Caldecott award books (from 1922 to the present), as well as a list of runners up. A children's librarian can check the books appropriate for any child.

Below is a listing of associations that publish various reading lists and offer excellent services in helping to choose appropriate reading material:

Library of Congress
Publishes an annual list of 100 current titles called Books for Children.

The Library of Congress
The Children's Literature
Center
Washington, D.C. 20540
(202) 287-5535

American Library Association
Association for Library Services to Children (ALSC) of the American Library Association publishes a complete list of Newbery and Caldecott winners and runners up. It also publishes an annual list of "Notable Children's Books."

American Library Association
Association for Library Services to Children
50 East Huron Street
Chicago, Illinois 60611

The Children's Book Council
Puts out a pamphlet called "Choosing a Child's Book."

The Children's Book Council
67 Irving Place
New York, N.Y. 10003

INDEX